D1447679

UNDERSTANDING HEALTH ECONOMICS

A Guide for Health Care Decision Makers

PAUL R McCRONE

KOGAN PAGE

To the Lord and my family

WX 138
Medical Economics

YOURS TO HAVE AND TO HOLD

BUT NOT TO COPY

Kogan Page Limited
120 Pentonville Road
London N1 9JN

© Paul McCrone, 1998

British Library Cataloguing in Publication Data

A CIP record for this book is available from the British Library.

ISBN 0 7494 2639 X

Typeset by Kogan Page Ltd.
Printed and bound by Biddles Ltd, Guildford and King's Lynn.

Contents

Series Editor's Foreword

Management can have a bad name in the NHS. We spend less of our budget on management than any comparable service and even that amount is being driven down. As the numbers of general managers in trusts are reduced, currently through a spate of mergers, more and more clinical time is taken up by management duties. Operational staff such as heads of specialist services or care homes, district nurses, ward sisters/charge nurses and their deputies find that they are increasingly expected to deal with management issues – the same issues that they were expected to refer to more senior staff just a few years ago.

The Healthcare Management Series is aimed at all staff who are involved in this process. People who have always thought of themselves as managers now find they must delegate more and more of their role as they take on ever broader responsibilities. Meanwhile, those who see themselves primarily as providers of care find they must lead and support a team of others, allocate scarce resources and make difficult judgements about priorities, if a high quality service is to be maintained. Basic training probably hasn't covered this; short courses on management may have been useful, but there is so much more to learn before feeling confident in this new role.

The writers of all the books in this series have been chosen for their practical experience of dealing with issues in the NHS and their ability to explain and illustrate the topics in a way which front line staff will appreciate. They are not, therefore, academic treatises but working handbooks full of advice and practical aids. More general books on management usually fail to reflect the particular features of the NHS, which make working in it both a joy and a frustration. The tribalism, the dominance of 'professionalism' and the commitment to the process of actually serving patients (rather than making a profit from them) which are such important drivers and which must be understood and harnessed if the service is to be well managed.

'Evidence based medicine' has progressed from being the mantra of a committed few to becoming established government policy supported by a national institute. Problems exist for both clinicians and general managers who fail to ensure the clinical effectiveness or safety of the practice in their organizations, yet finding and interpreting the necessary information can be extremely difficult. Judging its reliability and value requires a thorough understanding of the strengths and weaknesses of the methods adopted as well as a feel for the ethical and political issues.

Many decisions about the future of services and the way that they are provided are based on population studies about their 'worthiness'. If your service is threatened, how can you show its worth? If the person doubting the value of your work has figures 'to prove it' how can you challenge their case – find holes in their argument or find flaws in their methodology? On the other hand, you may want to make changes yourself and want to prepare a case to demonstrate their viability or to choose between various configurations of a service. Where do you start? What techniques are there available to you?

It was against this background that Paul McCrone rose to our challenge of producing a readable and practical book on healthcare economics to help people grappling with decisions about the best use of limited resources. Working with the author on this title has substantially changed the way I look at problems and think about the options for the use of resources to improve health. It has also made me more sceptical about some of the claims made for various services by their advocates.

A wider understanding and appreciation of what healthcare economics can offer will substantially improve the health of both the nation and the NHS.

Keith Holdaway
Head of Training and Development
Mayday Healthcare NHS Trust, Croydon

Chapter 1

Introduction: The Role of Economics in Health Care Planning and Appraisal

Economics has been described as the 'dismal science' because it is the study of scarcity. Most people would agree that resources indeed are limited, and this scarcity affects individuals, organizations and governments alike. It is a fortunate person who is able to purchase all that they desire with the income that they receive, and this also extends beyond the level of an individual. Economics has developed because there is a need to maximize the outcomes that can be achieved by deploying whatever resources are available. This is the essence of economic efficiency. Economists have often been seen as 'cost-cutters' when they should have been portrayed (or portrayed themselves) as 'outcome maximizers'.

Nowhere, of course, is the issue of scarce resources more emotive than in the health service. Here we are dealing with issues more crucial than whether or not to buy a second car. People's lives can be profoundly affected by the amount of health care which is available to them. Because health care is seen to be of great importance the demand for it is generally high, and some would say unlimited. This is increasingly the case, because technological advancement in health care technology means that we can do more now than ever before – a trend which is likely to continue.

At the time of writing, a new 'wonder drug' for impotence has

1

been announced which could potentially have beneficial effects for tens of thousands of people. However, it has also been stressed that if it were to be given on demand it would probably bankrupt the National Health Service (NHS). What can economics do to forward the debate about such treatments? It will be seen that economics is relevant not only in calculating the financial consequences, but also to ascertain the effectiveness and value of treatments, and can be a useful tool in determining their availability.

The expectations that people have regarding what health services can and should do are probably higher than ever before. Therefore, the problem of scarce health care resources will not disappear but will if anything become more pronounced.

In most industrialized nations, health care expenditure is between 5 and 10 per cent of gross domestic product (Figure 1.1). The United Kingdom has a relatively low level of expenditure on health care as a proportion of gross domestic product – about 6 per cent. This does not *in itself* mean that the UK system is underfunded. Abel-Smith (1981) considered that the UK health service 'is remarkably cheap compared with that of other nations of similar achievement' (p 373), and supports this argument by referring to the United States, Western Germany and France, which spent proportionally more than the UK on health but did not have lower rates of mortality.

In most industrialized countries there has been a steady increase (around one to two percentage points) over the last two decades in the amount of gross domestic product that is spent on health care. In the United States however, there was a large increase of 5.7 percentage points between 1976 and 1996. The escalating health care costs in that country have been one of the focuses for their policy makers and analysts in recent years. The issue of cost containment is one that is also addressed in other countries, although not to the same extent as in the United States.

There are a number of reasons why health care costs are rising. Many are particular to individual countries, and these cannot be dealt with here beyond the general observation that where health expenditure is based on budgets (as in the UK) rather than fees

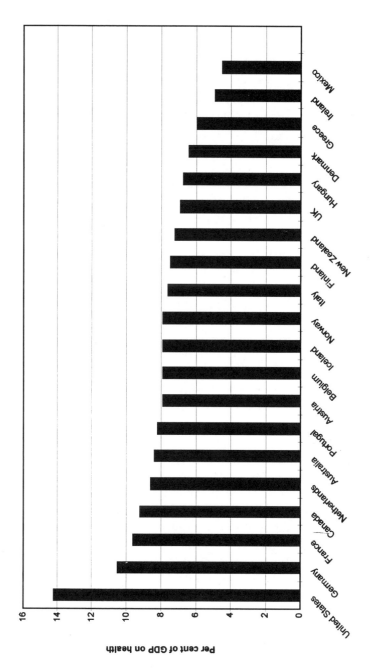

Figure 1.1 Per cent of gross domestic product spent on health care among OECD countries (source OECD/Crecles Software)

paid (as in the United States) cost containment is more likely (Abel-Smith, 1981). A general reason which affects all countries is that the aforementioned development of health technology is frequently expensive, and allows more interventions to take place. There is also an interesting proposition put forward by Baumol (1995) based on the fact that health care is relatively labour-intensive. Let us suppose that wages rise in the manufacturing sector because productivity has increased. This productivity increase means that the wage rise can be afforded without pushing prices up. If health care workers request a similar wage rise, which would be an understandable desire, this will not be matched by a similar productivity increase (because productivity rises faster in capital-intensive sectors rather than labour-intensive ones) and, therefore, overall costs will rise. In essence this means that as an economy develops, more money should be devoted to labour-intensive sectors (health, education etc) where productivity cannot increase as fast as in other sectors such as manufacturing. Increasing health expenditure as a fraction of GDP may therefore be a necessity.

Rising costs and needs means that hard choices often have to be made. In today's NHS this situation is very apparent. Rationing has become one of the main health care issues under scrutiny, even though it has been implicitly practised throughout the existence of the NHS. The move to a pseudo-market system of health care organization (particularly in the form of the purchaser–provider split and the emergence of GP fundholding) was developed – rightly or wrongly – as a means to achieve a more efficient use of finances. The proposed replacement of the internal market with purchasing by Primary Care Groups will not diminish this need for efficiency. Indeed an understanding of economics that is related to health care will be a clear aid to these groups.

Recognition of the scarcity problem in health care has spawned a subdivision of economics called health economics. Like its counterparts such as transport economics and environmental economics it is derived from economic theory *per se*. There are particular health care issues that make such a form of economics essential, and this will hopefully become clear throughout this book. There are a large number of health economists working in the UK, and one of the aims of this volume is to encourage the use of the subject and its techniques by those from managerial, clinical or nursing backgrounds. A number of other texts have been produced on the subject of health economics, but this volume is very much an introduction to the main ideas, and if readers wish to go deeper into the subject then they are recommended to refer to the works by Drummond *et al* (1997) and McGuire *et al* (1988).

Health economics really took off in the 1970s, and it is perhaps no coincidence that this was also the time when it became apparent that the post-war boom was over. Before then, when ideas of resource scarcity and rationing were not so relevant, economic input to the health arena tended to focus on issues such as hospital output, rather than on how resources should be distributed among different services. In 1981 it was noted with trepidation by Abel-Smith that 'The economic base from which health and social programmes are financed has been heavily eroded' (p 373). Since then health economics and health economists have proliferated, and much of the work conducted has been in the area of resource allocation. Although the search for economic efficiency has arguably been forced on to the agenda by circumstances, it should be recognized that careful allocation of resources needs to be sought after, even in times of relative abundance.

Health economics enables us to examine the burdens caused by illness and to choose between different methods of treatment. The principal aim of this book, which is written particularly for the non-economist involved in health care decision making, is to explain how informed choices can be made. This volume is not designed so that clinicians and managers can become economists. Rather it is to be hoped that many of the techniques (and much of the jargon) used by economists will become more accessible to those whose professional expertise lies elsewhere.

Different illnesses will frequently have unique levels of burden associated with them. Chapter 2 describes how the burden of illness can be measured in terms of cost, and discusses the relevance of such measures. There are a number of critiques of the typical method employed to cost illness, *the human capital approach*, and these are outlined. An alternative method, *willingness to pay*, is also described.

Economic evaluation is concerned with combining information on costs with that on outcomes. Costs may be defined as the values of activities that are foregone by choosing a particular option. This is explained in Chapter 3, along with a summary of what types of cost should be included in an evaluation. The way cost is measured is crucial if assessments are to be valid, and the chapter addresses this issue. Outcome can be measured in a number of different ways and these, to a greater or lesser extent, indicate the 'utility' that an individual attaches to a particular health state. The three main types of measure (monetized, disease specific and generic) are outlined in Chapter 4. One aid to health care evaluation which has arisen in recent years has been the quality adjusted life year (QALY), and its use, advantages and limitations are explored. There may be more than one way of choosing between competing interventions, and the main forms of economic evaluation are cost-minimization analysis, cost-benefit analysis, cost-effectiveness analysis and cost-utility analysis. Chapter 5 explores the advantages and disadvantages of these.

The need for evidence-based medicine appears to have been made central to recent discussions regarding health care planning. Closely associated with evidence-based medicine are prioritization and rationing. These terms are defined and their application discussed and the unique input that health economics provides for evidence-based medicine is demonstrated in Chapter 6. A critique is also given of the best-known prioritization exercise in Oregon.

The previous chapters will have equipped the reader with an outline of health economics and how it can be used to evaluate health care interventions. Chapter 7 brings this information together in a way which should enable an understanding of what to look for in such evaluations. The process of reform in the health service in the UK and elsewhere is likely to continue, although not necessarily in a constant direction. What the future holds is uncertain and health economics likewise should be adaptable to change. In the final chapter some issues surrounding the future use of health economics are addressed.

Throughout the text a number of case studies have been presented. These have been chosen primarily because they illustrate many of the concepts that are described. Many of the studies have originated from outside the UK, and it is hoped that this adds to their interest rather than limiting their relevance.

Chapter 2

The Cost of Illness

Illness is expensive. It is understandable that most people, when thinking about the cost of illness, focus on the monetary implications of providing the health services necessary to prevent and treat health problems. However, the consequences of ill health are also expensive to the individual, and their family or friends, in terms of pain, discomfort, fear and so on. The existence of illness will, in addition, frequently impact the ability of individuals to function in a way that they would in the absence of illness. This will prove costly if the foregone activity has some value, whether or not this can be measured. There are, therefore, many components of the *social* cost of illness (COI). However, given the practical difficulties in assigning monetary values to some costs, only a subset of these are included in most COI studies.

This chapter first outlines the most commonly used method by which illness is costed, and two case studies are presented to illustrate it. Next, we will question the relevance of such studies. A number of criticisms have been made of COI studies; these will be discussed towards the end of the chapter. For the purposes of readability, illness is used as a broad term to include disability, but it is recognized that the two are different concepts which are not always linked. COI studies use a number of economic concepts, some of which will be expanded in greater detail in subsequent chapters.

Estimating the Economic Burden of Illness

The methodology that has been used in most COI studies was described in detail in by Dorothy Rice (1966, 1967). In her seminal work, it was proposed that costs be measured for different diagnostic groups. A 'top-down' approach was employed where total health service expenditures were allocated according to the prevalence of different illnesses in the United States in 1963. In her calculations, Rice recognized that costs consisted of two components, direct costs and indirect costs, and made a number of important assumptions in calculating these, some of which have been challenged by others. The methodology described below has been supplemented with points raised by other authors endorsing such a process.

Direct costs

A number of services are used directly to impact illness, and these are primarily located in the health care sector. Rice cites the following activities that lead to these direct costs: prevention, detection, treatment, rehabilitation, research, training and investment. US expenditure for 1963 on hospital and nursing home care and the services of physicians, dentists and other health care professionals was divided according to the number of people treated in various diagnostic groups in that year. (Other health care expenditures, amounting to one third of the total, were not included due to difficulties in allocating across the different diagnostic groups.) Allocation between diagnostic groups was enabled by observing the relative levels of service utilization in a sample of hospitals, and applying these proportions to the total. Unit costs of individual services (described in Chapter 3) were assumed to be the same across the diagnostic groups, although the author recognized that this was not the case in reality.

This method allowed Rice to allocate all included health care expenditure, with no 'leftover' cost except for the one third which could not be allocated. For patients with more than one condition, only the primary diagnosis was used so that double counting could be avoided. For example, someone hospitalized with a primary diagnosis of angina, who also had a diagnosis of bronchitis, would only have a COI relating to the former *but this would include the services used due to the latter if treated at the same time.* If this were not the case then the services required for the angina would need to be separated from those due to bronchitis which would be difficult to do. (It will be seen later that this is a potential problem with COI studies.)

An alternative to the top-down method of allocating costs among all prevalent cases in a given year is to look at the lifetime costs associated with annual new cases (the incidence) of a particular illness (Hartunian *et al*, 1981). Incidence is less than prevalence when the effects of ill health exceed one year. The annual incidence of appendicitis is approximately equal to its prevalence as cases are treated and usually cured within a short time-frame. A different situation would occur with rheumatism, where the annual incidence is less than the annual prevalence because people generally have it beyond a year – there is an accumulation. Increased longevity can mean that the prevalence of many conditions may increase. However, this is not accounting for the fact that cures of illness will become more likely as time goes on. Using incidence figures in COI estimates involves predicting what future costs will be, and is seen as a 'bottom-up' method. For example, the lifetime course of angina, after incidence, could be estimated and service use and costs predicted.

Direct health care costs are typically associated with current medical expenditures to address the condition. However, the *outcome* of an illness will also affect direct costs in the future. Health care expenditures will be higher in the future if life is lengthened by treatment, and therefore these extra costs ideally need to be added to the cost of successful treatment, or subtracted from treatment which does not lead to an extended lifespan.

Indirect costs

People who are ill may be unable to perform roles which they would have undertaken in the absence of such a condition, or their performance in these roles may be compromised. This may be temporary when the illness is not serious and cured, or permanent for more chronic illnesses, including situations where the individual is institutionalized. The extreme case is when the illness is fatal. The resulting deficit in normal activity is an *indirect cost* because the economic burden occurs aside from treatment expenditures.

When this happens to working people, production is reduced as a result of work time foregone. These costs have long been recognized as important for society. Dublin and Lotka stated in 1930 that 'To let such deaths pass unprevented is, from the humane standpoint, a disquieting thought; from the standpoint of social economics it is, at the very least, a matter of inexcusably bad manners.'

Human capital approach

Frequently, economists have used the level of an individual's earnings to indicate the production potential foregone, and this is known as the *human capital approach*. It is based on the assumption that people demand the maximum wage for the skills that they have, but it is important to note that it is the cost to society which is relevant rather than the cost to the individual. Earnings are merely used to measure lost societal production. Rice followed this method, but felt that it was not ideal as some people who preferred to work in the public sector received lower earnings than their skills could command in the private sector. The gender and age distributions of those in different diagnostic groups were known and relevant earnings used. This meant that, in monetary terms, lost employment was valued higher for men than women. When this study took place mass unemployment was a distant memory and, therefore, it was assumed that in the absence of illness people would be economically active. However, there was some voluntarily and involuntarily unemployment, and the indirect costs were adjusted to take account of this.

Production losses were also included for individuals who had been engaged in domestic activities, but had had this affected by illness. The role of a 'housewife', to use the term of the day, was not rewarded financially in the form of wages and, therefore, the method which Rice applied to lost paid employment could not be

applied here. Instead she assumed that the activities that consti-
tuted domestic labour could in theory be 'sold' in the employment
market. Following on from this, the value of domestic labour was
taken to be equal to the wages paid to a formal domestic worker.

Other indirect costs have been described by Hodgson and
Meiners (1982). Patients will spend time travelling to and using services, and there may also be time commitments made by the family
of the patients in terms of caring and visiting. There may also be
detrimental effects on career progression if the individual returns
to work. Additional indirect costs occur if leisure time is foregone.

Payments of welfare benefits are not included in COI studies,
and in fact are not considered as costs in many other economic
analyses. This is because they are 'transfer payments' which are
used to redistribute income. Nothing is being produced in this way
and hence no cost occurs. Of course there is a financial cost, in that
money has to come from the treasury which could be used for
other purposes, but as these other purposes would often be transfer payments elsewhere there is no societal cost associated with
them.

The human capital approach goes further than an analysis of
one point in time, and assumes that the economic value of a person
can be estimated by the flow of earnings they will receive *during
their working life*. Anything which interrupts this flow will consequently result in a cost if the flow is not carried on by someone else.
The initial analyses of Rice examined production lost with a single
year. The methodology was subsequently adapted to take into
account lost future production, which would be a consequence of
particular illnesses (Rice, 1966). *Life tables* have often been used to
quantify the future flow of earnings to an individual depending on
his or her age and the expected number of life years remaining.
Dublin and Lotka (1930) used this method in calculating 'the
money value of a man', and noted that such tables date back at least
as far as 1853 and the work of William Farr.

The cost of future production loss was 'discounted' to present
values. This is because economists assume that a person would
prefer £100 this year to £100 next year, even after having taken
inflation into account. Similarly a production loss this year is more

costly than the same production loss in the future, because people are assumed to want to defer costs. A discount rate was used by Rice to reduce the value of future production losses caused by illness in 1963. Discounting will be discussed again in subsequent chapters.

Cost of Illness in the United States and Germany

The results of Rice's calculations are summarized in Table 2.1, alongside subsequent calculations for 1972 (Cooper and Rice, 1976). Comparing the amount that different diagnostic groups contribute to total illness costs showed little change between these years.

Table 2.1 Contribution of illness groups to total COI in the United States in 1963 and 1972

Diagnosis	1963, per cent	1972, per cent
Diseases of the circulatory system	22.4	21.2
Accidents, poisonings and violence	12.6	14.1
Neoplasms	11.3	9.2
Diseases of the digestive system	8.4	9.3
Diseases of the respiratory system	7.9	8.7

There is much international variation in the amount which individual illness groups contribute to total COI. Costs were calculated using the Rice methodology for 1980 in West Germany by Henke and Behrens (1986), and the five largest contributors to the total are shown in Table 2.2.

In the method used above and elsewhere, there was no attempt to attach a monetary value to the more intangible and subjective costs that occur with an illness. These are numerous and clearly important, but impossible to measure if this method is employed. However, another approach to costing illness, using the willingness to pay theory, does take into account such aspect of illness, and this will be discussed later.

Table 2.2 Contribution of illness groups to total COI in West Germany in 1980

Diagnosis	per cent
Diseases of the digestive system	18.8
Diseases of the circulatory system	14.8
Injuries	13.2
Diseases of the bones and organs of movement	9.6
Diseases of the respiratory system	8.4

Other Examples of COI Studies

Most COI studies have been conducted since Rice's methodological description, but a few do predate it. Dublin and Whitney (1920) conducted an early piece of work examining the cost of tuberculosis in the United States. Using life tables they calculated the effect on productive work associated with the hypothetical removal of tuberculosis. Attaching a dollar value to each working year lost, they estimated the total national burden to be US $26.5 billion (or US $500 million per year) *in the prices of that day*. This did not include the medical costs required to tackle the illness, or the extra costs that would be borne caring for people with an increased lifespan.

Case study: Cost of allergic rhinitis (hay fever)

In this study, by Malone *et al* (1997), the number of individuals who had had recent hay fever in the United States in 1987 was estimated from a survey of 14 000 households to be 26.7 million, including 12.3 million children. It was also possible to estimate the number who would have received medical care, and those who had their work or education affected by the condition. The survey included information on medication obtained and medical care contacts, and costs were attached to these. It was calculated that 11.5 million prescriptions for hay fever medication were made, costing US $184 million, in addition to 17.5 million medical contacts at a cost of US $524 million. Direct costs therefore amounted to approximately US $708 million.

In estimating indirect costs, the number of working days lost due to the illness (811 000) was multiplied by the individual's wage rate (based on the survey data); the resulting cost was US $37 million. School absence for children under the age of 12 (824 000 days) was costed according to the wage of the lowest paid parent, assuming that it was they who would take time off work to care for the child; this included zero values if the parent was not in paid employment. This amounted to US $13 million. The cost of lost schooling was taken to be zero for older children, where parents were assumed not to have to forego work. Some individuals would have their work activity affected but not stopped by hay fever, and the assumption was made that lost production due to this was equal to one quarter of the wage paid for a normal day's work. The resulting cost was US $17 million. Total indirect costs were calculated to be US $67 million for the year. Overall, hay fever in 1987 was estimated to cost the United States economy US $775 million, with 91 per cent of this cost due to medical contacts and medication.

The cost of hay fever was relatively low compared to the costs of other illnesses, which is to be expected given that for most people hay fever is not a chronic complaint and in-patient care is not generally part of treatment. The dominance of direct costs is caused by the fact that normal activity is seldom interrupted for long. It will be discussed later that the human capital approach, which was employed here, is not always valid when calculating indirect costs. However, in this case it was probably acceptable, as work loss is temporary, and may not be substituted for by other workers. Clearly there were costs that were not included (such as discomfort when hay fever occurred), which to the sufferer at the time might be considerable.

Case studies: Cost of mental illness

Much early COI work was devoted to establishing the cost of mental health problems. This was largely due to the fact that it was already perceived to be an expensive group of disorders because of the large number of hospital beds taken up by it (Fein, 1958), and that the indirect costs were likely to be high due to the chronic nature of specific mental health problems meaning that full economic participation would not be recovered in many cases (Malzberg, 1950). In addition, it was important to state the extent of the economic burden of mental illness at a time when the United States, United Kingdom and other Western countries were about to start to reduce the emphasis placed on long-stay hospitalization.

In 1963, the direct costs of mental illness in the UK were estimated to be £122 million (Association of the British Pharmaceutical Industry, 1965). Indirect costs, in terms of lost potential earnings, were not measured, but it was estimated that £17 million could have been claimed in sickness benefits for working days lost. These are equivalent to £1504 million and £210 million in 1995 prices. Recently, UK studies have examined the costs of a number of types of mental illness, some of which are summarized in Table 2.3. These figures are rough estimates, but do show that there is much variability between illness groups. What is concealed, though, is that *within* illness groups there are also differing estimates of the COI.

Table 2.3 Cost of mental health problems, original figures inflated to 1995 prices[1]

Illness	Direct cost	Indirect cost	Total cost
Alzheimer's disease[2]	£1 300m	not reported	£1 300m
Schizophrenia[3]	£500m	£2 000m	£2 500m
Neuroses[4]	£200m	£500m	£700m

1. The inflation of costs assumes that the structure and pattern of service delivery has not changed. This is clearly an unrealistic assumption, but is used here merely to enable the magnitude of economic burden to be approximated. Costs were inflated using an index of health care prices, but it is recognized that this is not the most suitable approach for the indirect costs of lost production.
2. Gray and Fenn (1993). The costs were inflated from 1990/91 prices, and the data is only for England. Indirect costs were not reported; the costs of lost production relating to the individual would have been negligible because most people with Alzheimer's disease would not otherwise be in employment. However, a substantial number of carers may have had to give up work early which would have large cost implications.
3. Davies and Drummond (1990). The costs were inflated from 1987 prices. Indirect costs did not include those due to premature mortality.
4. Croft-Jeffreys and Wilkinson (1989). The costs were inflated from 1985 prices. This only included the costs of patients presenting in general practice.

Purpose of COI Studies

COI studies, conducted according to the Rice methodology, do reveal the extent of health care expenditure on treatment and may indicate the potential productive activities foregone. Costs can be described at a national level, or for smaller units of analysis. For example, a district health authority may wish to estimate the economic burden of different illnesses within its catchment area. In addition it allows comparisons to be made between countries and over time. Is it useful, however, to show what these costs are? Economic evaluation can be described in terms of choosing between competing alternatives for our financial patronage. Do COI studies aid this in any way?

Cost of illness studies may facilitate economic comparisons of different conditions. This has attractions to those wishing to focus attention, and research money, on areas which are particularly resource hungry. It can also reveal areas which utilize high levels of resources which are not matched by proportional research investment (Serafetinides, 1991). For those with particular vested interests there are advantages in proving that their illness area is more expensive than others (Smith and Wright, 1996), and it is of interest that many COI studies have either been performed or financed by pharmaceutical companies who may wish to demonstrate the cost-reducing impact of a particular product.

Costing illness according to its prevalence may have particular use in a description of how health care expenditure is allocated, and clearly is an aid to political bargaining by those with decision making responsibilities at a macro level. Drummond (1992) suggests that incidence-based COI studies are useful in examining the progression of an illness over time, and for comparing the monetary effects of different treatment programmes. Such lifetime indicators of cost generated by the incidence-based method would, for example, enable public health professionals to show the long-term economic impact of eradicating or reducing a particular illness.

Disadvantages and Limitations

The method put forward by Rice and others has been criticized on a number of counts. Some of these have been more to do with the practicality of generating meaningful cost estimates, while others have been concerned with the theory lying behind COI studies.

First, when the prevalence approach is followed the presence of multiple diagnoses could lead to different costs than for single diagnoses. Rice allocated costs by primary diagnosis, thus removing the possibility of double counting. However, for conditions where comorbidity is common this would lead to distorted cost results. For example, it is known that substance abuse is relatively high among people with serious mental illness (Johnson, 1997). If costs were attached in the way suggested by Rice, schizophrenia would be more expensive and substance abuse less expensive than they are in reality. Whereas the prevalence approach is suited to the simultaneous calculation of illness costs for all diagnostic groups, the incidence method tends to focus on illnesses independently of each other. In the above example, costs of schizophrenia could be calculated to include all treatment costs for the condition itself plus those for related problems such as substance abuse. Substance abuse costs would include those for this subset of dual diagnosis patients also. If all illnesses were costed independently, but included costs of such comorbidity, the aggregate amount would, by definition, be more than the total level of health care expenditure.

Second, direct costs of illness have tended to be calculated only with reference to health services. While for most conditions this may be acceptable, there are others (particularly when the health problems affect everyday living) where services provided by non-health agencies are widespread. In addition, there will frequently be patient costs incurred as a result of receiving treatment, such as travel expenses, which may be considered as direct effects of illness. Chapter 3 will show that in some situations it may be acceptable only to cost inputs from one agency, but from a societal perspective all relevant costs should be calculated. Of course it is important to be pragmatic; some services may be used by such a small number of patients that the research time required in estimating costs would be too high but this should be (and sometimes is) stated in individual studies.

Third, some elements of direct cost are hard to divide between diagnostic groups, for example, hospital buildings, administration etc. When costs are required for a particular year it may be problematic to account for the costs of research, education and training which are investments for the present and the future. This is a practical difficulty with any costing exercise.

Fourth, direct costs in prevalence studies are usually obtained by dividing the total expenditure according to the diagnostic case mix in a given period. However, this assumes that the amount of money contained in a particular budget will all go towards treating or caring for people with a specific illness. It may be felt this situation should exist; however, it is quite feasible that on top of treatment costs are various administrative overheads, some of which will be directly relevant for treatment while others will not be. Also, in-patient costs will frequently be portrayed as an average figure for the entire hospital or ward, but patients will each require a unique level of input which this average cost will not pick up. This may not be important for hospitals or wards treating patients from the same diagnostic group, as at a national level differences will compensated for. However, for hospitals or wards with a variety of illnesses the average cost will be influenced by the number of patients with high input diagnoses, and this will cause less expensive illnesses to be over-costed. This is not a pedantic point as in-patient costs frequently account for a disproportionately high amount of total health care costs.

Fifth, there are ethical arguments against the use of the human capital approach in calculating indirect costs. Use of the technique means that women and people from ethnic minorities, who on average receive lower wages than white men, would appear to have lower costs of lost production. There would also be differences in the indirect costs according to the age of patients. If an illness attracted more attention on the basis of indirect costs it would be particularly favoured if it affected predominantly middle-aged white men. It also presupposes that illness is more detrimental for those on higher incomes. In the work of William Farr (1853), and cited by Dublin and Lotka (1930), there was a tenfold difference between the earnings of agricultural workers and those paid to 'persons in professions on moderate incomes' (p 44). The implication is that illness is more important for some people than others, which is surely an inequitable line to take.

Related to this is the assumption of a perfectly functioning labour market. If this existed then employees would be able to 'shop around' among a large number of employers until they achieved the wage that matched their level of productivity. It would not rise above this level because in such a market there would be no trade unions, and competition between workers would keep wages at the appropriate level. Clearly such a situation does not exist, and earnings are frequently below what they perhaps should be.

Sixth, the human capital approach assumes that, in the absence of illness, productive labour would be undertaken, which was not an unrealistic assumption to make in the mid-1960s. However, we all know that full employment has not generally been experienced in Western industrialized countries for some years, and there is a pool of people hoping to work who are able to substitute for those displaced by ill health. When this happens a nation's production is not affected beyond the period of employee replacement (Shiell *et al*, 1987). It is interesting to note that Dublin and Lotka recognized this in the United States in 1930, another time of high unemployment, although they still did propose the use of the human capital approach. Koomanschap and van Ineveld (1992) put forward the *friction cost method* of calculating indirect costs, where only the resources associated with replacement are included. They calculated the indirect costs of the incidence of cardiovascular disease in The Netherlands in 1988 to be 8 per cent of the costs measured in the traditional way.

However, the portrayal of indirect costs calculated by the human capital approach, even when overall there is no societal impact, can reveal the extent of the personal financial loss caused by illness. It has been argued by some that this will itself have societal consequences due to reduced consumption of goods and services. (If my earnings fall I will buy less goods which, other things being equal, will have a detrimental effect on those firms producing them).

Seventh, there are technical measurement problems associated with the human capital approach. Future life earnings, supposedly being a proxy for productivity, are calculated on a *current* cross-section of the population. Glied (1996) noted three sources of potential bias: the effect of real growth in earnings which cannot be observed from a population cross-section; the existence of specific current economic conditions, for example, high unemployment which will affect the number of people working and their level of earnings; and the size of different age groups in the current sample which could also be associated with earnings. Glied reported that predicted future earnings could divert from actual figures by as much as 50 per cent because of such biases. These difficulties do not themselves nullify the human capital approach but should be recognized as areas of potential inaccuracy.

Eighth, while production losses are likely to have the greatest magnitude, other indirect costs do exist which are usually ignored in cost calculations. These include foregone leisure activities, and the time spent by patients using services.

A ninth area of difficulty concerns the ease with which COI studies can be compared. According to Smith and Wright (1996) three particular aspects of the methodology need to be consistently applied for effective comparisons to be made between cost calculations for common diagnostic groups: prevalence estimates, rate of service use, and unit costs used. While there should be little dispute about the validity of these points it should be stressed that the latter two in particular would apply to comparisons between any economic evaluations.

Finally, the argument that COI calculations may lead to prioritizing of research and treatment initiatives is invalidated if the level of existing expenditure is inefficient or unwarranted (Shiell *et al*, 1987). In such cases less emphasis on these apparently high cost illnesses would in fact be required. COI estimates do not indicate whether care is provided in an efficient or effective way, and a number of health economists (Shiell *et al*, 1987; Drummond, 1992; Smith and Wright, 1996) have challenged the attention which is given to them on this basis.

There appears, therefore, to be a number of important theoretical and practical problems with typical COI methodology. This is particularly so for indirect rather than direct costs, which is a good reason for reporting these separately (Drummond, 1992). However, there have been a vast number of such calculations (Shiell *et al*, 1987). This is perhaps due to the political impact of being able to state how much a particular illness costs.

Willingness To Pay Approach

An alternative way of costing illness is to use the willingness to pay (WTP) approach. This will be discussed in detail in Chapter 4, but in short can be defined as a way of depicting the COI, from either a patient's or society's perspective, which takes into account otherwise non-monetized effects of illness. It may be that the traditional way of calculating COI reflects the lower limit of the willingness to pay estimate (Kenkel, 1994), but only if it is accurate and theoretically correct, about which there is some doubt. Use of WTP in costing illness has not been used extensively. One particular problem with it could be that it is possible that inconsistent values will be generated for common illnesses (Glied, 1996). However, it will be seen that it is conceptually correct, whereas the standard method has theoretical shortcomings but is more readily formulated.

What Questions Should Be Asked of a COI Study?

There are important disadvantages associated with COI studies, but the number of studies shows no sign of abating. If they are to be of use certain important questions must be asked by health care decision makers. First, have costs been calculated according to the prevalence or incidence methods? This has important implications for the study's relevance given the context in which the decision maker is working. If COI studies are used to examine care provided to current patients, then the prevalence method is required. The incidence method is more appropriate for lifetime costs, and would be of interest for preventative interventions. Second, how have illness costs been measured? Economic costs of illness are not necessarily the same as those included in budgets and accounts. This will be discussed in some detail in the following chapter. Third, have all direct costs been included? It may be that non-health service inputs are used to treat illness and these should be considered. Fourth, what indirect costs have been calculated, and would these in reality be reversed in the absence of illness? If not, then they may not be caused by it either. Finally, what can such a study do to meet such aims as increased or stable service financing, research activity and the efficient allocation of resources?

Summary

COI studies have proliferated since the work of Rice in the 1960s. They do not inform us about how resources *should* be allocated because they do not address the issue of efficiency of care provision. It will be argued in subsequent chapters that the question of efficiency should be addressed by a cost-effectiveness analysis or one of its variants. However, COI studies are not without use. They do give an indication of the value of resources used to treat an illness, whether effectively or not. As such they can be used to focus attention on the evaluation of services in this area, but low cost illnesses may be no less worthy of attention. Indirect costs estimated by the human capital approach only show the value of foregone productive resources if these can not be replaced. COI studies are interesting and have some uses but these are limited, and there do exist concerns regarding their theoretical underpinnings. Health care decision makers should not be unduly influenced about the 'economic burden' of any illness, but should seek out evidence concerning the most efficient way of treating it.

Important Points For Health Care Decision Makers

- COI has a direct (medical care and social care costs) and an indirect (foregone work) component.
- The prevalence approach to costing illness relates current costs to current diagnostic mix.
- The incidence approach to costing illness relates future costs to current new cases.
- COI methodology is limited particularly for indirect costs.
- COI studies have some use but should be treated with caution.

Chapter 3

Cost Measurement

The previous chapter described the way in which illness may be costed at a high level of aggregation (in economic terms, the macro level), and critiques of this method were discussed. Fundamental to such studies is the measurement of cost. It will be shown in subsequent chapters that there are a number of different ways of conducting evaluations of health care programmes, but cost is crucial to them all. It is imperative therefore that we know what we mean by cost, and that we ensure that it is measured accurately and appropriately. This chapter will first give a definition of cost, and then go on to explore which costs are relevant, and how they are measured, reported and used. A number of case studies will be presented to illuminate the discussion.

What is Economic Cost?

Cost occurs when a productive activity takes place, which necessitates the use of scarce resources that could be used for some other purpose. For example, the provision of a breast cancer screening programme will require the services of medical staff and premises, which could alternatively be used for a children's immunization clinic. In the introductory chapter it was stated that there are not enough health care resources to meet every health care need and, therefore, the provision of one service will reduce the potential provision of another. There is consequently a cost.

Economists describe this as an *opportunity cost*, as there is a lost opportunity whenever the resources used could be focused on some other activity, and it is the value of this 'other' activity which determines economic cost. It should be apparent that some (indeed most) unpaid activities will also have an opportunity cost. If I devote my leisure time to watching a football match I am deciding not to use it reading a book or some other activity which would also have some personal value to me. I cannot do both adequately at the same time. These alternative leisure activities would have a value even if it were hard to monetize them, and as such there is a cost associated with the chosen activity. There are some resources which may not in some circumstances have any cost. The air we breathe is abundant in supply – my breathing it does not deprive anyone else of it and therefore its cost is zero. Leisure time spent in one activity may be 'worthless' if there really is nothing else we would wish to do with that time. However, most activities will have an opportunity cost, and health care provision perhaps has more instances of such costs than most other areas due to the high and growing demand for it.

It is important at this juncture to distinguish opportunity costs, as described by economists, and outlay costs which are more relevant to accountants. The former are steeped in the science of scarcity – scarcity leads to choices which lead to costs. Accountants view costs as financial expenditures necessary for the provision of activities at a particular time. Both are valid in specific contexts, and should perhaps be viewed as overlapping concepts with much common ground. The differences occur mainly because of their individual applications. With regard to the previous chapter, an accountant would prefer to adopt the prevalence approach to costing illness where the total level of expenditure is distributed between its component parts (there should be no expenditure left over), whereas the economist would perhaps favour the incidence approach where only those costs that occur due to activities undertaken for that illness are measured (there may be some expenditure left over). The two may coincide but often will not (Drummond, 1980). Outlay costs exist because of money, whereas opportunity costs would still prevail in the absence of money. (This is portrayed effectively by groups of individuals who barter with activities such as babysitting and music tuition.)

The fact that opportunity costs and outlay costs are different concepts can appear academic, in that the former are most often treated as if they were equal to the latter due to the complexities of any other method (Knapp, 1993a). However, the difference is important in terms of what is costed and what is not when evaluating services.

What Do We Cost?

In identifying which costs are relevant, it is first necessary to know from whose perspective they are to be calculated. Most economists would wish to examine the impact that illness, or an intervention designed to treat it, has on the whole of society. Health care resources used in one way are at the expense of their use in other ways – not just within the health care sector. If the amount of public expenditure on the National Health Service increased in real terms then it would have to do so at the expense of other areas such as defence or education, unless taxation also increased (of which there is a practical and political limit). It was emphasized in Chapter 2 that there exist direct and indirect costs, and both of these ideally need to be calculated in an evaluation.

It is important, therefore, to adopt a comprehensive approach to costing (Knapp and Beecham, 1990). However, sometimes it will be known that the vast majority of treatment costs are caused by particular service inputs. In such cases it may be possible to calculate costs for just these (Knapp and Beecham, 1993). This road should be trodden with caution though, as any new or changed intervention could have unexpected consequences on peripheral services which would go undetected if only a core group of inputs were costed. Also different conditions will be more appropriate to this method than others (Whynes and Walker, 1995).

When focusing on a particular health care intervention, it should be realized that there may be direct consequences for non-health budgets. For example, the costs associated with a treatment for angina will include medication and contacts with nurses and cardiologists, but also the inputs from home helps and other social care specialists, required due to reduced ability to do everyday tasks for some sufferers. Any change in a treatment programme may affect costs for different agencies in a number of ways. This is particularly relevant in the case of community care, which is mainly provided by health and social services, but may also involve education, employment and legal service inputs. Therefore, from a neutral point of view it is necessary to take a wide view of economic costs.

Neutrality is not going to be always prevalent though. You may be reading this book as a health service or social services manager and, although recognizing the importance of the wider impact of illness and the measures used to combat it, will be particularly interested in the cost implications in your sector, and in particular your hospital or department. This is understandable. Economic evaluations can be used to focus on particular sections of the economy, and findings will be relevant to those working in these areas, but the limitations need to be recognized. When used in an evaluation (see Chapter 5) one might be able to say 'treatment A represents better value to the NHS than treatment B' but not 'treatment A is more efficient overall than treatment B' without examining *all* relevant costs.

The agencies on whom costs fall do not just extend to those formally established. Informal carers (friends or relatives) may play an important part in the care process, as will the patients themselves. The time that patients spend receiving health care has an opportunity cost, even though the refusal of such care could have serious implications. From an economic standpoint patients are as much a producer in the health care process as doctors and nurses (Hart, 1995). The previous chapter explored the indirect costs of lost production due to illness. When these do exist, and it was seen that there are reasons for thinking that they may be overstated, a treatment intervention may reduce (or increase) this loss. Consideration of these cost implications also needs to be made.

What costs are relevant?

Whatever perspective of costing is adopted, the criteria for selecting which costs to include is the same. In costing an illness, any activities that arise because of the illness should be included. In an economic evaluation, when a health care intervention is compared with either doing nothing or with an alternative procedure, then any activity that could be affected by the intervention should be costed; activities which it is known will not be affected do not need to be costed. It is the costs that can change which are of interest. Essentially we should follow the maxim: if it moves cost it, if it doesn't then don't.

This needs to be qualified by thinking back to opportunity cost. Drummond (1980) makes the point that the notion of opportunity cost requires that anything that has an alternative use should be costed even if there is no financial outlay for it. Conversely we do not need to cost activities that are affected by the intervention but whose resources have no alternative use and are valueless. (If such activities exist, they are few in number.)

Most studies, including those discussed in Chapter 2, do not include welfare benefits in cost calculations; they are transfer payments representing a shift of money from one group of people (taxpayers) to another (the recipients). Nothing is being produced by them and there is no cost to society. However, if one were to focus on the implications to the patient rather than society then they would represent a negative cost (or gain), and if we looked at the treasury they would be a cost (Drummond *et al*, 1997). The way we treat welfare benefits in cost calculations is characteristic of whether an economic (exclude them) or financial (include them) definition of cost is applied. In practice we need to know the financial burden of illness *as well as* the economic consequences.

How Is Cost Measured?

In the discussion so far there has been an emphasis on the opportunity cost of choosing one activity over another, which leads to the occurrence of a cost. However, in reality those planning and managing health care will be more concerned with which service expenditure can be increased or decreased, rather than 'all or nothing decisions'. Absence of public investment in types of health care is rare and tends to be confined to non-essential treatments, for example, some cosmetic surgery. It is decisions at the *margin* for which economic evaluation is generally useful, and *marginal cost* is particularly relevant.

Marginal cost is the cost of producing one more output of health. It is quite possible, indeed it is probable, that this marginal cost will differ from the average cost. An example will help to illustrate this divergence. Let us consider a hypothetical immunization clinic aimed at people going on holidays abroad, based at a local health centre. The service initially plans to vaccinate 25 people each week. The cost of a vaccine is £4, one quarter of a nurse's time is spent running the clinic and this amounts to £80, and the capital cost of the building which is devoted to the clinic amounts to £60 per week. Therefore, the total weekly cost of the clinic is £240 per week (25 patients multiplied by £4, plus £80 plus £60). The average cost is £9.60 (£240 divided by 25 patients). Let us assume that a company in the area gives their workforce an unexpected bonus, and the number of vaccinations required for one particular week rises to 40 because of increased holidays. It is assumed that one busy week will not entail more staff being taken on or larger premises being required. Therefore, the total cost is now £300 week (40 patients multiplied by £4, plus £80 plus £60). The marginal (or extra) cost for each of these 40 patients is £4 – the cost of the medication itself. The average cost is now £7.50 (£300 divided by 40 patients). Therefore, the total marginal cost of providing 15 extra vaccinations is not £144 (15 patients multiplied by the original average of £9.60), but rather £60 (15 patients multiplied by £4). Marginal costs will frequently be less than average costs, and if changes in activity are to take place it is the marginal difference which is crucial. Here we have looked at the cost of 15 more units of output. Essentially marginal cost is the cost of one more unit being produced (£4), but in this simple example it was constant and so applied for each of the 15. The difference between two different modes of operation, or two different services, is the incremental cost difference, and this is particularly relevant when costs are combined with outcomes.

It is also important to consider the working capacity of a service. In the health care sector, it is often the case that services are running at full capacity and have waiting lists for patients requiring care, although there are also the cases where hospital wards have not been used due to limited funds. If a service is running at full capacity then any increase in numbers treated will entail a cost. If a service is not running at capacity the cost will be less.

The above example calculated the marginal cost of health care provided. However, it is often more meaningful to focus on health achieved. In the following case study the marginal cost of achieving a specific output rather than the administration of the associated intervention is of interest

Case study: Repeated testing for colonic cancer

In this often-quoted study by Neuhauser and Lewicki (1975), the marginal cost of testing for colonic cancer was calculated, and compared to the average cost. The starting point for the analysis was the assumption that in a population of 10 000 people there would be 72 people with colonic cancer. A second assumption was that occult blood would be identified in 91.67 per cent of cases when a test was performed. A second test would identify 91.67 per cent of missed occurrences (100 per cent – 91.67 per cent) from the first test, and so on. The overall percentage of cases detected would increase as more tests were performed even though each individual test would have the same success rate. Six sequential tests would detect 99.9999 per cent of occult blood occurrences. Of the 72 assumed cases, the accumulated number detected after each test would be 65.9, 71.4, 71.9, 71.939, 71.9417 and 71.9420. The increment is reduced after each test because most cases have already been detected.

The authors assumed that the cost of the first test was US $4, and the following five were US $1 each. Positive tests led to the administering of barium at a cost of US $100 to clarify the results. The total cost rises after each test, but at a reducing rate due to the falling numbers of positive results requiring barium. The total costs after each test would have been US $78 000, US $108 000, US $130 000, US $148 000,

US $163 000 and US $176 000. The average cost is this total cost divided by the number of true positive results and this also rises (from US $1 175 to US $2 451) but by diminishing amounts. The marginal cost is the change in cost after each test divided by the change in outcome. Therefore, the marginal cost of the second test is US $30 000 (US $108 000 minus US $78 000) divided by 5.5 (the increase in the number of positive results) ie US $5 500. However, because the change in outcome after the *sixth test* is so small (0.0003) the marginal cost of detecting occult blood is immense at US $47 000 000 (US $13 000 divided by 0.00030). This is about 20 000 times the average cost!

The reason for the difference between average and marginal cost in the above study is due to the fact that it examines the marginal cost of a positive test result from the sixth test, not the marginal cost of actually administering the test. In the example of the vaccination clinic both the average and marginal cost figures would have been very different if we had focused on the cost of avoiding a particular illness rather than administering the vaccination.

Ideally we do need to cost services at the margin. However, it is difficult to do this and average costs are frequently used. In the short run this may lead to inaccuracies. In the long run all costs are variable as premises can be changed, equipment bought and salaried staff taken on. In the example of the vaccination clinic, if the increase had been permanent then, assuming the service was running at full capacity previously, there would need to be an increase in staff time and perhaps capital costs. Consequently, *long run marginal costs* may well be similar to average costs. As health care planning should be undertaken with more than a short-term perspective, average costs can be acceptable.

Measuring service use

Once the relevant services have been identified, they can be measured and costs calculated. In measuring service use, it is important to choose an appropriate time period,which will be representative of the services being received. This may be straightforward in the case of a brief intervention such as a tonsillectomy, where the service from beginning to end can be measured. It is not often practical to measure service use in this way where the treatment is particularly prolonged – for example, recovery from stroke – or maybe permanent, for example, care for diabetes. Therefore, it is necessary to use a period of time which encapsulates the range and quantity of services used. If it is too short, important care inputs might be missed. Conversely, if the period is too long and the service measurement is retrospective, errors could be made about what services were actually received during the period.

Accurate measurement is important, but particularly so for services which might contribute a disproportionate amount to total cost. This may not be known beforehand, in which case equal care must be taken with all measurements. On the other hand in many areas of health care it will be known that in-patient care, for example, is particularly expensive and so should be measured as accurately as is possible.

Unit costs

When service use data has been collected, it will be necessary to combine it with appropriate cost information. Ideally we would wish to obtain the opportunity cost of providing a service, ie the value of those resources in their best alternative use. As this is not readily available the costs that are generally used are those which prevail in the market place, for example, earnings. We have also seen that the concept of marginal costing should be adhered to; but it was mentioned above that average costs may be acceptable to use if it is assumed that they resemble marginal costs in the long run. How are these calculated? Two steps are necessary:

The starting point is to calculate the total cost of a service input. This is the level of expenditure which is required to make that input operational. For example, the total cost of a health visitor consists of their salary, the pension and national insurance contributions made by their employer, overheads for office space and administration, and travel expenses. Costs for other personnel would be similar in their composition. Services such as in-patient wards consist of the above staff costs and also food, heating, laundry etc. This latter group of items are known as *hotel costs*.

For services which use buildings or equipment, capital costs will need to be calculated, in addition to staff and other costs. Here the principle of opportunity costs serves as a useful guide. The money used to buy or rent property or a piece of equipment could in theory be invested in a savings account and earn interest. The opportunity cost therefore is the interest that would otherwise accrue over the period equal to the lifespan of the property or equipment. This final figure can then be converted into a cost per year. This is known as an annuity. Allen and Beecham (1993) report that the annuity of a building which would cost one million pounds to replace is £61 867, assuming it to have a 60-year lifespan, and using a 6 per cent interest rate. Incidentally, this procedure is different from that used in calculating purely financial costs, which would focus on the value of the resources depreciating.

When comparing studies, it is important to ensure that the same elements of cost have been included; otherwise these comparisons will be erroneous, although this may not matter that much if only low cost services differ. The total cost figure used in the development of unit costs will of course depend on whose perspective is relevant. It is important that this is specified as differences can be substantial (Wolff *et al*, 1997).

Services for which there is no financial payment will usually still have an opportunity cost. As no exchange of money takes place, such an opportunity cost is defined in terms of a *shadow price* (Robinson, 1993). For leisure time that is given up in using services, Drummond *et al* (1997) suggest that the value could be set equal to zero, to the average wage rate, or to the average wage rate plus overtime earnings. They feel that the latter is most appropriate as it is the price that an employer would have to pay to buy leisure time off an employee. However, they also point out that the convention is to give leisure time a zero value, and that the effects of a non-zero value should be determined through a sensitivity analysis. (Sensitivity analyses are used when assumptions have been made about particular variables in an evaluation, and an examination of the results when these assumptions are changed shows the degree of sensitivity. The role of sensitivity analysis will be discussed in subsequent chapters.) A problem with using earnings-related values in costing leisure time occurs when patients are unemployed. This may be a consequence of illness, or the labour market in general – a problem encountered when using the human capital approach.

Volunteer time and informal care can be valued in the same way as non-employed time. An alternative is to look at the services which are being provided and to see what level of earnings they could command if sold in the market. For example, if a relative or friend visits a patient once a week and provides a range of domestic activities, then this might be valued at the same rate as a home help.

The second stage of costing is to divide the total cost by the number of service outputs produced. The type of such a measure will depend crucially on the specific evaluation being undertaken. For example, in-patient costs may be described in terms of cost per patient day, week or episode; staff time can be divided into appointments, hours, and even minutes. Differences between studies in these units of measurement can also make comparisons problematic.

A difficulty arises if the service for which a unit cost is required provides inputs for more than one client group, or delivers different types of service. For example, a single unit cost for an accident and emergency department will necessarily be an under- or over-estimate for many patients due to the great variation in conditions being presented. Wolff *et al* (1997), observing that community mental health centres often provide a number of services, stress the importance of calculating a separate unit cost for each distinct activity.

Methodological divergence will lead to different unit costs being reported. A number of reports on the unit costs of GP services were reviewed by Graham and McGregor (1997). They found that the cost of a 10-minute consultation ranged from £3 to £11 in 1995/96 prices. Comparison between studies is clearly hindered by such inconsistency. While ideally the same (correctly calculated) unit costs should be used in all studies, the least that should happen is the reporting of unit costs that *are* used. A number of unit costs for health and social care have been published by Netten and Dennett (1997), and these are revised regularly.

Once appropriate unit costs have been measured, they can be multiplied by the quantity of service received. An error in either of these two components will affect the final results and any conclusions drawn from them.

Discounting costs

Some costs will be prolonged. We have seen above that in some studies it will be necessary to choose a representative period over which to measure service use. However, it also needs to be recognized that future costs will have less value than current costs, even after ignoring the effects of inflation. If we can delay paying for something then we usually will. (Conversely, health benefits will be desired sooner rather than later.) This is known as *time preference.* Any perusal of newspaper advertisements for electrical and furniture goods will reveal the same principle at work, ie buy now pay later. Because of this, future costs and benefits need to be *discounted* which entails reducing the value of each future period's costs by a specific percentage. These future values are then represented as a current value. The Department of Health has suggested using a discount rate of 6 per cent. It has been suggested by Krahn and Gafni (1993) though, that discount rates should reflect the perspective from which costs are being calculated. Discounting is only necessary for interventions for which there are future costs. Therefore, the costs of removing wisdom teeth will not generally require to be discounted. However, the costs of kidney dialysis will.

How Is Cost Reported?

There are numerous papers in medical journals which contain evidence of service costs. We have seen above that calculations need to be accurate and consistent. Assuming they are, it is important that they are displayed in an accessible and informative manner.

It is common to find that the mean cost of a health intervention is presented. This is useful in that it allows us to calculate the total costs of different numbers of patients treated. For example, if it is known that the mean cost of a heart transplant is £30 000 then, other things being equal, 10 transplants will cost £300 000 and 20 £600 000. (It is assumed here that the increase is in the long term and the service is already running at full capacity and, therefore, staff and capital costs will have to increase.) However, the mean will only be informative if the distribution around it is equal. A mean of £30 000 would be representative of five patients with the following costs: £10 000, £20 000, £30 000, £40 000, £50 000.

The mean cost will usually have been generated from a sample of costs for different patients receiving a transplant. Let us assume that four patients cost £25 000, but one cost £50 000 due to complications during surgery, making it more prolonged and thereby requiring more surgeon and nurse input. The mean cost is still £30 000 (the sum of each operation divided by five) but it is misleading because most of the patients had operations costing £5 000 less than this. The most expensive operation has the effect of increasing the mean cost and making it biased. The median (the mid-point in the distribution) and the mode (the most common value) is £25 000, which would be a better indicator of the cost of someone else having a transplant. (The median is more useful than the mode, because the latter will only be helpful if a reasonable number of patients do have exactly the same cost.)

However, it will still be appropriate to use the mean in estimating the costs of another, say, 100 operations if complicated operations are likely to be repeated at the same rate. The mean therefore accounts for *outliers* which the median does not, and outliers will generally reoccur. Which measure is best to use then? There is no definitive answer, and both should ideally be reported, and used when appropriate: the median for showing typicality and the mean for extrapolation, if the sample from which it is drawn is representative.

Any average measure of cost, whether it be the mean, median, or mode, will still conceal information as to the distribution of cost among patients. It is useful to have some single measure of dispersion, such as the standard error or standard deviation, or a range (for example, confidence intervals or an interquartile range). A straightforward diagram showing the distribution of costs is very rarely produced, and yet is informative. For some areas of health care a highly skewed cost distribution will be common, particularly when a small number of people receive in-patient care, and this needs to be accounted for in any analysis of cost data (Gray *et al*, 1997).

Cost-variation analysis

When assessing the costs of two or more different health care interventions, it may be possible to compare the averages and say that A is more expensive than B. However, within A and B there is likely to be a range of costs, and an exploration of this may have implications for the allocation of resources. It may also be the case that we have only one intervention and no comparisons, and therefore analyses are confined to within-group differences.

Such analyses are possible by developing what economists call a *cost function* (Knapp, 1993b). Traditionally a cost function simply relates resources to outputs, ie as the quantity of output changes so does cost. Here we are concerned with all factors that in reality may relate to cost. Changes in health outputs will be among these factors. If high blood pressure is reduced then this may have been associated with a high level of health care inputs. (It may be the case that such an improvement in outcome will also lead to a decrease in future levels of service use and costs.) However, the costs associated for cardiac care may also be explained by age, gender and lifestyle factors (diet, exercise, smoking etc). Such correlates of cost can be identified using statistical techniques like multiple regression models. These quantify the impact that each predictor has on the variable in question, in this case cost. An example is given below of an analysis of variations in the cost of providing renal dialysis in the United States. Costs were measured for different provider units rather than individual patients.

Case study: Variations in the costs of providing renal dialysis care

The authors (Dor *et al*, 1992) collected cost and other information from free-standing centres which provided care for patients with end-stage renal failure. They wanted to identify factors which explained variations in the total costs of running the services. Five possible products were defined: home haemodialysis, haemodialysis in the treatment centre, continuous peritoneal dialysis at home, and training for both types of home dialysis. The mix of these products was expected to have an impact on a centre's costs and, therefore, the numbers of patients using each product were used as potential cost predictors. In addition, the wages paid to staff, patient population demography, and whether the centre was 'for-profit' or not were tested to see if they predicted cost. Results relating to individual factors are not presented here, but it was shown that the range of variables could explain (in other words predict) between 71 and 77 per cent of cost differences. The results enabled estimation of the cost of each of the individual products, and it was revealed that some of these differed markedly from the amounts that the government paid to providers through the Medicare system.

The above analysis was developed specifically to examine the financing of renal dialysis in the United States. As such it is not directly relevant to the UK. However, this method of exploring variations in hospital costs can be applied here, and this may become more important with the use of casemix measures of hospital activity, such as health care resource groups, to finance providers.

Use of Cost Information

Chapter 2 provided details of how illness itself can be costed. If arguments about the alleged inappropriateness are put to one side, it should be apparent that good quality cost data is required for such studies to aid those drawing on their findings.

The calculation of costs is a fundamental part of economic evaluation, ie assessing if a particular health care intervention should be chosen, or expanded or decreased. However, costs on their own, while of interest, rarely allow us to do this. Low costs are not necessarily synonymous with efficiency; the least costly procedure (in terms of direct but not indirect costs) is usually to do nothing, which is hardly efficient. It is unfortunate that economics has been seen as focused on costs, which are only one side of the health evaluation equation. Costs must be analysed *alongside* health outcomes, and economists can be involved in the latter at least as much as the former. The following two chapters will take this further.

Management of health care services requires the flow of accurate and useful cost information. In the UK this is particularly so since the NHS reforms established a separation between purchasers and providers; if health authorities or GP fundholders were to buy services they would need to know the cost and also believe that it was appropriate. In the late 1990s, the NHS is set to undergo more change with primary care groups being responsible for purchasing patient care. Whether or not one agrees with past or present reforms, it is clear that decision making is becoming more overt, and cost data needs to be able to meet the needs of different players in the health care field.

One tool available to health care managers in the UK since the early 1990s has been the health care resource group (HRG). This casemix system, based on diagnosis-related groups (DRGs) from the United States, allocates hospital in-patients into groups according to their primary diagnosis. If patients within the groups have a similar (or equally distributed) length of stay, then they can serve as proxies for cost evaluations. Accurate cost information attached to HRGs could be a possible aid to health economists who otherwise would have to conduct time-consuming cost calculations (Whynes and Walker, 1995). However, HRGs are sometimes only a rough indicator of service use and contain a number of limitations which need to be addressed, and they are mainly concerned with in-patient care (Royce, 1993).

Summary

This chapter has defined cost in terms of opportunities foregone, and this applies to services and other inputs whether or not they receive a payment. Prior to the measurement of cost it is crucial to know from whose perspective it is to be done. Once this has been established then all activities that may be affected by a new service, or by a change in an existing one are costed. The ideal measure of cost is at the margin; in the short run this will frequently be different to average cost, but may resemble average cost in the long run. We have seen that the process of costing involves measuring service use, and applying it to relevant unit costs. Costs that are generated in the future should be discounted.

The presentation of cost data is perhaps as important as its accurate calculation. Substantial cost variations may exist, and a simple average measure will leave much cost information hidden. It was also emphasized that costs, properly formulated and presented, are but one crucial element in an economic evaluation.

There can be a preoccupation with making cost and economics synonymous. Cost is simply a way of describing resource utilization which leads to outcomes being produced. This will be taken further in the following chapter.

Important Points for Health Care Decision Makers

- Costs represent the value of foregone opportunities by undertaking particular activities.
- Costs should ideally take a societal perspective, but in practice may relate to particular agencies.
- Marginal costs are more appropriate than average costs, but in the long term these may be similar.
- Market prices are usually used as a proxy for opportunity cost.
- Future costs have less value than current ones and should be discounted.
- Cost variations need to be explored.
- Economic evaluation requires the combination of costs with outcomes.

Chapter 4

Outcomes

It may appear that economics is predominantly concerned with costs, and the work of economists has indeed often been concentrated on this area. A review of medical journals will frequently reveal that clinical evaluations have had cost components 'added on', sometimes in an attempt to satisfy funding agencies. However, economics is at least as relevant to outcome as it is to cost. This belief is hopefully justified by defining exactly what is meant by outcome from an economist's standpoint. This chapter will go on to explore various ways of measuring outcome, and will have direct relevance to the following chapter which examines ways in which outcome and cost can be synthesized.

What Is An Outcome?

In arriving at a definition of outcome that is relevant to health economics we will briefly cover two elementary areas of economics: production theory and consumer preference. It will be seen that health economics draws these two concepts together in a particular way. No attempt is made to be comprehensive in this outline, but rather the concepts which are of particular interest to health economics are identified.

Anyone embarking on a study of economics will at a very early stage be faced with 'the theory of the firm'. In essence this tells us that firms produce an output, and in order to so do they use inputs such as raw materials, machinery and labour. The amount of production that takes place will depend on the availability and price of these inputs, and also the price which the firm can charge for their product. If they are producing two or more products, then these factors will also determine how much of each is made. For example, a pharmaceutical company might produce antidepressants and also a new form of painkiller. Let us assume that the demand for the former is higher and that it requires less expenditure on inputs. The profit gained from such a product will be potentially greater than for the painkillers, because the price gained from it will be relatively high due to its level of demand, and its costs will be less. It is this product that will be concentrated on if the firm is a *profit maximizer*. (In the real world, of course, companies will manufacture a wide range of products in order to capture as much of the market as possible.) What the firm produces is its output, which we will call 'outcome'.

Production theory is of great significance to health care evaluation, as interventions should be chosen or expanded on the basis of the relationship between what is achieved and what this achievement costs. Expensive treatments which do not produce positive health care outcomes should not usually be chosen in preference to low cost ones where the outcomes are large. Economic evaluation is concerned with establishing what choices need to be made between these two extremes.

Health gain

In health care we are mainly concerned with health itself as an outcome, and it is here that health economics departs from traditional producer theory. *Health services* are of secondary importance to *health gain*. People who are ill only have an intermediate desire to use health services as a way of achieving their real goal which is health gain.

Utility

In making the assumption that health gain is important rather than health care itself, we need to explore the idea of *consumer preference*.

43

This is founded on the principle that individuals are *utility maximizers*. Varian (1987) points out that utility used to be defined as a measure of someone's 'well-being' but, because this is rather an abstract idea, utility now is just a way of depicting the preferences that people have for different goods and activities. Consumer preference states that individuals will prefer product A to product B if they derive more utility from it. The fact that utility is difficult to define does not preclude its analysis, because the preferences that are determined by it can be observed by choices that are made. This is perhaps a long-winded way of saying, 'I don't know what it is about apples, but I do like them more than oranges.' The different aspects of an individual's utility will be contained in their *utility function*. The same principle can be applied to health care, although here the 'well-being' definition is quite relevant. This can be seen by the fact that many health economics studies which seek to estimate utility do so by measuring quality of life.

When presented with a range of health states there would undoubtedly be some we would prefer to avoid than others; in other words we could rank them (this concept is known as ordinal utility). We have earlier said that health gain is the outcome which we are interested in. More generally we are interested in the *change* in utility that occurs as a result of a health care intervention, ie we want not only to order our health states but we want to measure them and any changes in them (cardinal utility). A number of elements may be included in the utility function of someone receiving health care, such as a cure of an illness, the ability to work, reduction in fear and a decrease of pain. In addition, the process of service use (time loss, discomfort during treatment etc) may affect utility.

If we were to choose between a range of health care states to be in (or to most avoid), then we could attach a weight or value to each one, and use this weight in evaluative exercises. The practical exercise of choosing between health states may appear to lack purpose until we realize that this is inevitable for those funding and delivering health care. If purchasers knew how residents in their catchment area valued different health states then the decision making process could be enhanced. The same would be true if the utility of actual patients were ascertained following different types of treatment.

Therefore, we can see that the product or outcome which should be maximized (subject to cost) is health gain from one health state to another. By measuring the difference in utility of two health states separated by time we are calculating health gain. Some health states have higher utility than others, and it is to these which most weight should be attached.

The individual is both the producer of health gain as well as the consumer of it (Hart, 1995). This theory has some logic. There are a number of activities which lead to health gain or health deterioration, and use of health care services is just one of these activities. This is particularly so in the public health arena where lifestyle factors are just as important as the provision of health services, in affecting the level of heart disease, for instance. Social and personal investment activities such as education and income have also been shown to have an impact on health status (Auster *et al*, 1969).

Economists are primarily concerned that health care should maximize utility. However, economic evaluations of health care interventions commonly measure outcomes in one of three ways: monetary, clinical effectiveness or utility. The first two may or may not represent the utility that a patient gains from an intervention. The latter in theory does, but there is not total agreement as to how utility should actually be measured. In some instances outcome does not need to be measured, and this will be expounded in the following chapter. Obviously economists are only one of many professions involved in evaluating health care interventions, and in many cases the outcome measure will need to be determined by clinical staff. This does not imply a conflict of views – clinicians will favour measures that best show the effects of an intervention which by definition will be inputs to a utility function. The measure of outcome which is chosen will determine how the results from any evaluative exercise can best be used.

Monetary Outcomes

We have seen in Chapter 3 that costs are valued in terms of money, which makes sense as service provision usually entails some financial burden. However, it may also be possible to measure outcomes using monetary units, and this is intuitively appealing as utility measured in pounds or dollars is relatively straightforward to analyse.

Human capital approach

Which health care outcomes can be measured in financial terms? The most applicable outcome is increased or decreased production. The main method by which this has happened has been to adopt the human capital approach which was discussed in Chapter 2. This entails calculating the value of production which occurs as a result of a health care intervention, and requires estimating the expected stream of income that remains to an individual during their life compared to people who do not have that particular illness. Likewise, any effects on the productive capability of friends or relatives can be estimated in this way. Changes in health status following some treatment can also affect the future utilization of health care services. These can then be costed and used as outcome measures. If the monetized benefits run into the future, a discount rate should be used as described in Chapter 3 for costs. The case study which follows describes the way in which monetary outcomes were estimated for three different types of treatment for vitamin A deficiency.

Case study: Treatment for vitamin A deficiency in the Philippines

Lack of sufficient vitamin A is particularly harmful for children. It can cause a disease called *xerophthalmia* which can lead to blindness and be fatal, and can lead to other infectious illnesses. It is most prevalent in developing countries where nutritional problems may occur. In this study by Popkin *et al* (1980), three different interventions were evaluated. Children were given either a high dosage of vitamin A twice a year

in the form of a capsule or they were given monosodium glutamate fortified with vitamin A, or their communities were exposed to a health
education programme. While xerophthalmia-related blindness and
mortality were virtually eliminated by each of the three different treatment programmes, they were less effective in reducing related problems, such as infectious diseases which could affect the production of
the people in the area. The monosodium glutamate was most effective
(83 to 85 per cent of cases), followed by the high dosage capsule (75 per
cent) and the health education programme was least effective (50 per
cent). The potential benefits of these options, to be measured financially, were increased lifetime earnings, and reduced health care treatment in patients who were successfully treated.

The level of future earnings in relation to xerophthalmia was seen to
depend on which of four scenarios an individual was in. First, they may
have the illness but not die or go blind (1.75 per cent of children). Second, they might go partially or totally blind as a result of the illness
(0.015 per cent). Third, they might die from the illness (0.44 per cent).
Fourth, they may not have the illness, but be at risk of other communi-
cable diseases from other children with it (97.8 per cent). The expected
lifetime income resulting from each of these scenarios was then subtracted from expected income in the absence of xerophthalmia – the difference being the gain from completely eliminating the illness. (Clearly
the gain in income resulting from avoided deaths would be greater than
avoiding blindness, where the loss of production would not be total for
all individuals.)

This potential gain in income was multiplied by the probabilities of
belonging to each group (which the above shows was extremely low
with the exception of the fourth group), and the expected income from
eliminating the disease was obtained by adding these products. These
benefits were then multiplied by the probability of each intervention
being effective.

Out-patient costs associated with the disease would be reduced
were it to be eliminated, and this potential reduction was also included
as a benefit. However, the authors did not include the possible
increased health care utilization associated with longer life as an element of social cost.

Benefits were discounted because they would largely accrue in the
future. It was shown that the fortified monosodium glutamate produced the greatest monetary benefits, mainly because it reduced
related infectious diseases most effectively which increased the total

production of individuals *without* the primary illness. This is an interesting finding – health care was having most impact on those without the illness. While the health education programmes had the least economic benefits, it was recognized that they would have dealt with other issues not included in this analysis.

The above case study is a relatively thorough application of the human capital approach. However, the criticisms made in Chapter 2 to this method are applicable here. In particular, there is no guarantee that in the absence of illness production would have taken place and therefore the benefits are possibly biased. If people are known not to be in work then the human capital approach would suggest that they experience no benefits from health care. Other benefits have not been included in the evaluation, which is a common problem with such analyses. Outcomes such as improved quality of life, which would undoubtedly be caused by the elimination of blindness, are not readily costed, leaving increased production and reduced service costs as practically the only benefits which can be included. Most benefit was due to potentially increased production by those without the disease, a finding which can be challenged ethically and, because of the human capital approach, also theoretically. Measurement of benefits in this way can, at best, only partially illustrate the utility gained from health care interventions.

Willingness to pay approach

Another method of attaching monetary values to health care benefits has arisen in recent years which should be more closely related to the utility which is gained or lost. This approach is known as willingness to pay (WTP), and was originally developed for use in assessing the benefits of environmental projects but is suitable for health care evaluation (Donaldson, 1993), and is being used increasingly. Using this approach, health benefits are measured by finding out how much individuals are willing to pay to achieve them.

The idea of WTP is generally understandable as it is a concept utilized whenever goods are bought. For instance, there is a maximum amount of money we would pay for a newspaper. If we actually end up paying less than this then we have made a personal gain (known as consumer surplus). In valuing health, WTP does not typically require that money actually exchange hands, but that individuals express their utility gained from a health state as if such an exchange did occur. As such it is an attempt to simulate 'missing markets' (Drummond *et al*, 1997).

If we buy a newspaper we are attaching a monetary value to such benefits as the information we gain from it and the enjoyment of doing the crossword. The price we are willing to pay may also reflect disutility – for example, ink left on our hands – and a political stance with which we might disagree. Clearly we do not *explicitly* weigh up all of these considerations in our minds as we make our way to the newsagent's, but *implicitly* they are likely to hold.

Whereas the human capital approach is limited in the benefits measured, WTP theoretically includes all aspects of an individual's utility function. If we have a maximum amount that we would be willing to pay to achieve a particular health state, then this should be determined by elements of our utility function. This would include negative aspects of health care (Gafni, 1991), such as side effects of treatment. These and other elements of utility cannot be objectively measured, but WTP does allow them to be subjectively valued. Because it is inclusive in what it values, WTP is an attractive concept (Muller and Reutzel, 1984).

WTP is a sound theoretical way of valuing benefits (Johannesson and Jönsson, 1991), but it is not always simple to apply. Two main options are available to determine how much a person would be willing to pay to achieve a given state of health: revealed preference or expressed preference (Johannesson *et al*, 1996). With the first of these, actions that actually do take place are observed to illicit WTP values. For example, if someone wants to avoid stress and to do this chooses to work in a rural area for less pay than they could achieve in an urban setting, then this pay differential reflects their revealed willingness to pay to avoid stress. However, a number of factors will usually influence where someone works and the pay that they receive, and revealed WTP may therefore be limited in scope. The fact that health care in the UK is not paid for at the point of use is another limit to this method.

The second way of conducting WTP, expressed preference, is where individuals are surveyed and their *hypothetical* WTP recorded. Questions may be open-ended; for example, 'What is the maximum amount you would be willing to pay for laser treatment for myopia (short-sightedness), if it has a 50 per cent success rate?' Or they may be discrete; for example, 'Are you willing to pay £400 for laser treatment for myopia, if it has a 50 per cent success rate?' Open-ended questions may be aided by a bidding game. Here the questioner starts off with a high (or low) amount and then gradually decreases (or increases) it until the amount the individual is willing to pay is ascertained. Alternatively, randomly shuffled payment cards can be given to the respondent who then chooses the most appropriate one. A disadvantage of open-ended questions is that the respondent is faced with a particularly unreal situation. While payment for health care could feasibly occur, a range of different prices would be unlikely. Also, when using the bidding game, the starting bid might influence the end value given. Discrete questions are answered 'yes' or 'no' and, therefore, resemble most goods that are actually paid for. Different prices would be presented to separate groups of individuals and, assuming a particular distribution of responses, an average willingness to pay can be deduced. This is becoming the preferred method, but requires a large sample of respondents. It does not though reveal any one individual's maximum WTP.

It should be realized from the above that the way in which questions are posed will have a crucial impact on the results gained from WTP studies. The context of the questions is also of importance. It has been suggested by Gafni (1991) that WTP be elicited with reference to a hypothetical insurance scheme. This would entail, for example, asking respondents how much extra premium they are willing to pay to cover the possibility that they may incur a particular illness. This would be a more realistic scenario where insurance schemes are commonly used. In the NHS, health care is paid for mainly out of taxation revenues, and a suitable question may be to ask how much extra taxation people are prepared to pay for certain medical procedures to be provided. An example of this is provided by Olsen and Donaldson (1998) and summarized in Chapter 6.

It has been stressed by a number of authors that all people (or a representative sample) who may possibly benefit from health care should be asked to state their WTP. This is in line with maximizing the benefit to the whole of society. However, most studies have focused on the amount that patients themselves are hypothetically willing to pay.

A growing number of WTP studies in health care have been conducted. Early ones tended to focus on the amount that individuals would be willing to pay to avoid fatal conditions. However, because WTP should be well placed to measure utility (which includes many aspects of care) there is now more diversity in its application. The following example examined the amount that people were willing to pay to have a chronic, but not fatal, disease cured.

Case study: Willingness to pay for cure from rheumatoid arthritis

This relatively early exposition of the WTP theory in health care, by Thompson (1986), involved 247 individuals with rheumatoid arthritis being confronted with the hypothetical possibility of a complete cure. The treatment to achieve this would not be included as part of any insurance policy. The individuals were first asked if they would pay any extra than they were doing at present for this treatment. If this was so, they were then asked to state the maximum percentage of their family income that they would be willing to pay for such a treatment. In order to obtain considered responses, a third question asked whether they would be able to live adequately on their remaining income; the WTP amount could then be revised. It was recognized that some answers might be particularly irrational, and therefore any zero percentages stated (after the initial question indicating if they were willing to pay extra) were ignored and any over 50 per cent were set at this level. Over 80 per cent of responses were felt to be rational. The mean WTP expressed as a proportion of income was 22 per cent, and this was similar for different groups defined according to educational attainment. The author noted that in making their decisions, individuals tended to focus on the effect that a cure would have on their functional ability.

The response rate was high in this study, and it was claimed that this was due to the style of questions and the skill used in administering them.

The above case study overcame the impact that income might have on the amount people are willing to pay by asking for the *percentage* of income. This approach was supported by the fact that there was very little difference according to education. A difficulty with the study was that people were presented with an unreal situation – there is no medical cure for arthritis. The value expressed by individuals is not particularly useful unless treatment is available. (It may though be useful if used to prioritize further curative research.) Only people with arthritis were questioned, and therefore the values expressed do not necessarily reflect those of society in general.

As WTP allows many aspects of utility to be included in a valuation, it may be particularly useful when attributes of an intervention have consequences aside from medical decision making. In the example below, WTP was used to estimate the value that women placed on ultrasound for normal pregnancy.

Case study: WTP for the benefits associated with ultrasound

This study was conducted in the United States by Berwick and Weinstein (1985), who recognized that some health care interventions – for example, ultrasound – had medical and non-medical benefits. With ultrasound, medical benefits could be in terms of enabling informed decisions to be made by doctors to maximize the health of the mother and the baby, or by reassuring themselves about the progress of the pregnancy. The latter aspect would be a benefit with no decisional implications. Likewise, parents could make practical decisions following an ultrasound (what colour to paint the baby's bedroom, employment etc), or the ultrasound could benefit them in a non-decisional way (the provision of a photograph, reassurance about the baby's health etc). It would be expected that parents would value their own benefits and those accruing to the physician.

A focus group of women who had previously had an ultrasound identified a number of attributes that women would potentially value.

These related to information concerning the baby's health, the mother's health, the birth date, whether twins were expected, the gender of the baby, seeing the image of the baby, and the provision of a photograph. Sixty-two women who either had received, or were receiving, prenatal care were interviewed, and asked to state the maximum they would be hypothetically willing to pay for an ultrasound, and for each individual attribute of it.

Table 4.1 Summary of WTP for ultrasound results

Actual cost of ultrasound	US $65
WTP for whole test	US $706
WTP for each attribute, added up	US $1 217
Contribution of decisional attributes to WTP amount	74%
Contribution of medical attributes to WTP amount	63%
Contribution of non-decisional attributes to WTP amount	26%
Contribution of non-medical attributes to WTP amount	37%

Table 4.1 shows that there was a huge difference between the amount that the ultrasound test actually cost and the amount that women would *hypothetically* be willing to pay for it. The women in the sample gave most weight to attributes that would aid decision making and would provide medical benefits. However, the amount that the women were prepared to pay for attributes that were not of a medical nature and those that did not have decision making implications were still valued substantially. The authors concluded that economic evaluations which did not include such attributes as outcomes would not be complete.

The study just described used WTP to value definite medical benefits plus those that would be likely to have no medical implications. The following case study used the discrete choice method of WTP to measure the value placed on different methods of antenatal care where outcome was assumed to be identical and, therefore, qualitative attributes were of primary relevance.

Case study: Willingness to pay for antenatal care

Measurement of antenatal care benefits lends itself particularly well to WTP. Care given to pregnant women can be either GP/midwife led or consultant led. There are practically no differences in outcome either for women or their children, but certain aspects of the care process (information, location, choice etc) may be preferred if provided in one of these ways rather than the other. Ryan *et al* (1997) wanted to discover how much pregnant women were willing to pay to receive such treatment options, and used a discrete choice form of questioning (yes or no answers). The study sample (numbering 936) had already been allocated to one of the care plans, and were asked if they would be willing to pay a fixed amount for the service if it were not available on the NHS. The fixed amount was one of 20 possibilities (sent out in roughly equal numbers), ranging from £25 to £10 000.

Using a statistical model, certain factors that were potentially associated with saying 'yes' or 'no' to the price asked were examined. Not surprisingly, the higher the price the more likely would be a negative response. Older women were also less likely to accept the price asked. Those on higher incomes found the price they were asked more acceptable. The type of antenatal care that the women were actually receiving made no difference to the answer given. By analysing the distribution of yes/no responses, the mean willingness to pay could be computed. Overall, women were willing to pay £2 467 for antenatal care. However, there was no statistically significant difference between GP/midwife led care or consultant led care. This seemed to imply that the respondents did not attach great importance to differences in the care process. However, the authors felt that WTP may not have been sensitive to such differences. This may imply that WTP itself is not an appropriate way of determining utility values. However, the fact that the technique is used for everyday transactions suggests that the methodology of studies, particularly how questions are formulated and interventions described, should be refined.

Another concern that they had was that the technique used to calculate mean WTP is substantially influenced by the amounts of money referred to in the questions that individuals are presented with, and the number of different bids that are sent out. This is because individual respondents are faced with only one price to which they will or will not agree. The different individual values that were distributed would have to reflect the likely pattern of values that people would in reality be willing to pay, and to determine whether this is achieved is far from easy.

In theory, the way in which a health care intervention is delivered should influence the overall utility that an individual gains from it, and it would be expected that utility gain might be reflected in the amount someone is willing to pay. The above study did not support these assumptions though, and reasons why this might be so were mentioned. However, it may be the case that such *process utility* does not in reality exist. In a study comparing keyhole and conventional surgery for gall bladder removal (Donaldson and Shackley, 1997) half the patients in a sample were offered descriptions of the outcomes of each option, while the other half received information about outcomes and process. From an objective viewpoint, keyhole surgery was felt to be superior in outcome (less time in hospital and time off work, and less pain) and process (smaller incisions, no stitches required, smaller scars). However, when the two groups were asked how much extra they would be prepared to pay for keyhole surgery compared to traditional treatment, those with information about outcomes but not process gave a higher amount. Given the supposed process benefits of keyhole surgery, this was unexpected. The description of how keyhole surgery was performed seemed more precise than for conventional surgery, and the authors felt that the provision of items of information about which patients might have negative thoughts could cause such a result. This is perhaps a worrying finding as it suggests that providing patients with full information about their treatment may cause them to value it less – even if it is superior to less effective but more straightforward interventions.

A problem with WTP applied to health care is that individuals may object to the whole idea of paying for health services other than through taxation or insurance. WTP is concerned only with the value attached to health by individuals, but obviously those conducting research need to be aware of, and sensitive to, any understandable misconceptions that may arise. The results of a WTP study could in theory be used as the basis for policy makers implementing charges, but this would be a misuse of the concept. Many of the WTP surveys that have been conducted have included qualifying statements, which stress that individuals will not be asked to pay for their health care as a result of their response. It is felt that this increases the response rate and reduces protest answers.

An alternative to willingness to pay which may be more attractive in some circumstances is willingness to accept (WTA). Individuals are asked for the minimum amount of compensation that they would accept if they were to suffer from a particular health state. This is perhaps more relevant to environmental and transport policies where particular projects may have damaging effects. However, the increase in medical litigation, particularly in the United States but also in the UK, indicates that individuals may demand compensation in the event of certain medical circumstances.

As both WTP and WTA aim to measure utility, where both can be applied they should come up with the same answer. However, this is frequently not the case. One study (Dubourg *et al*, 1994) estimated the amount that individuals would be willing to pay for relatively low risk of non-fatal traffic accidents. They were also asked to state how much compensation they would be willing to accept for a higher risk. It was found that WTA values were higher than WTP values. In fact the lowest WTA amount was higher than the highest WTP amount. The authors felt that there were difficulties in the way in which individuals attached values to these scenarios. However, even accounting for this, there was still much unexplained disparity between the two methods.

It can be seen that WTP and the human capital approach are quite different ways of attaching monetary values to outcomes. The former is theoretically superior in that it can (but might not) reflect all aspects of a person's utility function, whereas the human capital approach by definition only includes certain elements of utility, particularly the ability to work, and it may miscalculate these. WTP may not be as readily applied as the human capital approach. However, the advantages of WTP should be kept in mind, and more studies should use it and endeavour to overcome its operational difficulties.

Disease Specific Measures

Most evaluations of health care, which may or may not include an economic component, measure outcomes in terms specifically defined by the category of illness being treated. For example, in comparing different medication options for epilepsy we may want to measure the number of seizures which occur during a defined period of time. Clearly, such disease specific measures of outcome are likely to be clinically meaningful and relevant. The number of seizures would have been preferable to measuring the level of electrical activity in the brain, which may or may not have led to seizures. The latter type of outcome measure, electrical activity level, can be described as a surrogate endpoint (Johannesson *et al*, 1996) as it is not likely *in itself* to affect the utility experienced by a patient. Since certain aspects of health (cholesterol levels etc) are associated with health problems (heart disease etc), surrogate endpoints are not invalid as outcome measures, but more concrete measures should ideally be used (heart attacks prevented etc).

If outcome is measured in a disease specific context it may not be clear what aspect of outcome to measure. Drummond *et al* (1997) suggest that when measuring the effectiveness of a health care intervention, it must have one clear aim, or the intervention must achieve all of its different aims. In this way the effectiveness (or ineffectiveness) of an intervention is not in doubt. Practically these criteria may be difficult to achieve. With schizophrenia, the aims of community care interventions may include improving functioning, reducing symptoms, and increasing the quality of life of patients and their families. However, it is often the case that only the latter of these is achieved. A more pragmatic approach may be to say that when there are multiple aims, effectiveness is achieved if any outcomes are positive and none are negative. More pragmatic still is that the positive outcomes outweigh the negative outcomes.

There may be a number of different instruments designed to measure the same aspects of health care. These will usually have slightly different emphases, and will also vary in validity and reliability. A good example is the large number of quality-of-life measures. In choosing from among a range of instruments, it is important that the health care decision maker appraise the use of potential instruments where they have been used elsewhere.

The main disadvantage of effectiveness measures that focus on particular illness groups is that they do not allow comparisons to made across specialities. In an issue of the journal *Evidence Based Medicine* (vol 3, no 2), which summarizes research findings published elsewhere, a specialized stroke unit was shown to be more effective than standard care provided on general medical wards in terms of survival, the proportion of people who were able to live at home, and their level of independence (Indredavik *et al*, 1997). In the same issue, catheters covered in antiseptic were shown to be more effective in preventing infection than standard catheters (Maki *et al*, 1997). These two treatments both improved health, and therefore potentially increased utility. As such they are of importance. However, there is no way of comparing the utility increasing potential of one against the other as disease specific measures of outcome were used.

Generic Measures

Generic measures of health care outcome are crucial in comparing across different disease categories. This is clearly important in the UK where those who decide (essentially health authorities or GPs) which health care interventions should be chosen, increased or decreased do so from a vast and diverse range. In order to compare the outcome achieved from, for example, kidney transplants and measles vaccination, a non-disease-specific method is required. The most frequently promoted of these is to use quality adjusted life years (QALYs). These have been developed over a number of years, and their use described in an influential paper by Weinstein and Stason (1977).

QALYs are designed to combine two theoretically independent components of utility – length of life and its quality. It is possible to use just life years saved as a measure of outcome, but this would be totally ineffective in dealing with interventions for non-life-threatening conditions. Of course in some situations, and particularly in countries where early mortality is high, it may be preferable to choose only between those health care treatments that do prolong life.

For many health problems, such as heart disease and cancer, the provision of treatment is essential in order to prolong life. However, it should be apparent that much, or indeed most, health care is devoted to improving the quality of life of patients. For example, in the case of terminal cancer, palliative care can greatly enhance the quality of life for patients and their families. Other illnesses may not be life-threatening and therefore it is only the quality of life which is affected by treatment. QALYs are used to value health states experienced over a certain length of time; as such they can also quantify the changes which occur due to treatment. Clearly, quality of life is a subjective concept, and it is in its definition and measurement that most of the QALY development and controversy has been focused. Quality and quantity of life are together assumed to be a proxy for utility, as all medical care outcomes can potentially be measured by them. However, they do not measure process utility (the utility or disutility gained from the actual use of a service) and, therefore, are not as comprehensive as WTP.

One QALY is assumed to be equal to one year's life in which quality is maximized, and one year's life where quality is not maximized is taken to be a fraction of this. For example, if someone has a stroke they may feel that their quality of life has deteriorated to half the level it would have been if the stroke had not occurred. This means that over ten years they will experience five QALYs (10 multiplied by 0.5).

Measuring quality

A number of ways have been developed to directly measure the quality of different health care states. The approach that is probably the most grounded in economic utility theory is the *standard gamble*. This is rather complex to use, and is most easily understood from an example.

Suppose that, for the purposes of a health care evaluation, we need to know the value that a person with chronic asthma attaches to their quality of life. A treatment option is presented to them which has two possible outcomes: either full health for the remainder of their life, or death. The person is free to choose either the treatment or to remain with chronic asthma. If the probability of full health is equal to one, ie no chance of death, then we would expect the person to choose the treatment option. It may be the case that with treatment the probability of full health is 0.99 with a 0.01 chance of death. It is likely that many would still opt for the treatment. However, there would be a point, for example at 0.80, where the individual is indifferent between the treatment and remaining in their current health state. Obviously, this would depend on patient characteristics, and how risk averse they are. Some people would not choose the treatment option at all if there were any risk of death associated with it. However, we would expect that a greater risk of death from treatment would be accepted if the prevailing condition caused relatively high levels of distress.

The probability level at which the individual is indifferent between treatment and no treatment is the quality of life weight that is given to that health state for that individual. The possibility of death as a result of the treatment option is rather a stark comparator for some health conditions. An alternative is to use some pre-defined level of poor quality of life. However, this would make difficult any comparisons with types of care which could prove fatal, as different end points are used.

Similar, but more straightforward, to the standard gamble technique is the approach known as *time trade-off* developed by Torrance *et al* (1972). Here the person with chronic asthma would be asked to state how many years of full health they would accept as a substitute for, say, ten years with chronic asthma. It is assumed that they would choose between zero and ten years. The proposed number of years would be decreased or increased until a point of indifference was reached. If they said that they would accept eight full health years, then the quality of life value for their current state of health is simply eight divided by ten, ie 0.8. Although this method is quite understandable, it is not rooted in utility theory as closely as the standard gamble technique.

A concept that is like the time trade-off method, but more controversial, is the *person trade-off*. Here, the respondent is asked to say whether they would choose one treatment over another, and they would make this choice based on the health conditions and numbers of patients using each treatment. The numbers would be altered until an indifferent response was attained. It might appear distasteful to compare numbers of people treated in this way, but it could be argued that this is what implicitly happens whenever a certain intervention is chosen. It should also be remembered that changes in health care programmes are often conducted at the margin, ie rather than one intervention being chosen instead of another, it is likely that one is increased rather than another. Is it unethical to increase one area of health care expenditure just because another is not increased?

Much more simple is the *rating scale* method. Here individuals are asked to rate their health state, or a hypothetical one, along a straight line with defined end points (usually full health and death). Assuming that full health and death are indicated by unity and zero respectively, the quality of life weight is determined by the distance on the line the point is from these extremes. One problem with such a method is that people may have a tendency to select a point near one of the extremes, or in the middle. Also, if more than one health state is being rated then there may be a tendency to spread the responses out evenly, which might not reflect actual preferences.

Magnitude estimation asks respondents to say how much more or less they prefer one health state to another. I might feel that my quality of life is twice as bad when I have flu than when I have backache. This does not give immediate quality of life scores.

These methods may result in different scores for the same health conditions, and this is a cause for concern (Nord, 1992b; Stavem, 1998). QALYs potentially have the advantage of being a way of comparing diverse health care states, but not if estimates of quality of life scores are inconsistent. This is important to bear in mind whenever consulting QALY league tables (see Chapter 6). Many assume that the standard gamble is the most theoretically correct way of eliciting quality of life weights, but the time trade-off has been proposed as more acceptable (Nord, 1992b; Johannesson *et al*, 1996), and some view it as more theoretically correct (Richardson, 1994). The rating scale approach is most easily administered and may be preferred for large studies (Froberg and Kane, 1989).

Multi-attribute scales

Ideally one of the above methods of determining the utility which an individual attaches to a health state should be part of any evaluation of treatment options using QALYs. However, this is not always practical. A number of multi-attribute scales have been developed which provide a short cut to deriving utility scores. One that has been used particularly in the UK has been the index of health related quality of life (IHQL). The current version of this (Rosser *et al*, 1992) comprises eight levels of disability, five levels of pain and five levels of distress. A series of weights between one and zero have been estimated for different combinations of these attributes and as such participants in a health care evaluation need only to state which level is relevant to them on these three attributes.

More elaborate is the EQ-5D instrument, and its use has been described by Kind *et al* (1998). This was formally known as the EuroQol, and consists of five domains (mobility, self-care, usual activities, pain or discomfort, and anxiety or depression), each of which have three levels (no problem, moderate problem and extreme problem). Combinations of these domains allow 243 health states to be valued. It also contains a global measure of quality of life in the form of a visual analogue scale (a form of rating scale) ranging from zero to 100.

Other instruments that have been widely used are the Short-Form 36 (Ware *et al*, 1992; McHorney *et al*, 1993) and the Nottingham Health Profile (Hunt *et al*, 1989). The former appears to be relatively sensitive in detecting less serious health problems than other measures (Brazier *et al*, 1992; Essink-Bot *et al*, 1997). Such scales are more easily administered than techniques such as the standard gamble or time trade, but they do rely on the predetermined weights being appropriate to the question in hand, and it can be the case that they are insensitive to particular illnesses (Hall *et al*, 1992). Instrument design is of great importance (Carr-Hill and Morris, 1991). There is a trade-off between the generalizability of multi-attribute scales and the sensitivity of directly measured quality of life. Health care professionals will need to choose a method of measuring outcome that is feasible given the time and money constraints that influence evaluation itself, while ensuring that the relevant questions are answered.

A question arises as to whose health state rating is relevant. In direct estimates of utility, patient-determined values are generally used. However, if the broad social outcomes of a health care intervention are to be considered then all people who could benefit from treatment should be included, and a representative sample of all members of society may be applicable. This question has important ethical and social considerations. There is no clear-cut answer, although the tendency has been to focus on patient benefits over and above those accruing to society as a whole.

Once a health state has been given a weight according to one of the above techniques, then it can be combined with expected length of life to arrive at a QALY score. Length of life is simply taken to be the average number of years that a person in the given health state is expected to live, which may or may not be less than that of someone in full health.

Quality of life is likely to change over time and QALYs have to reflect this. Weights have to be calculated according to each phase of an illness. Another related point is that the quality of life for a *specific* time may be affected by the expected course of illness. Normand (1991) gives an example of one person with an illness experiencing a year of high quality of life, followed by death, compared to another person with an illness who has a poor quality of life during that same year but recovers. If we were to look only at that one year then we would choose the first health state, other things being equal. The author suggests that the weight given to that year should reflect the fact that knowledge about the likely outcome of the illness is influential. If utility at one point in time is determined in part by what has gone before or what the prognosis is, then a more 'holistic' way is required to measure outcome (Hall *et al*, 1992).

Health care that maintains a particular health state may be disadvantaged if compared to others using QALYs. Care for often chronic conditions, such as arthritis, may not result in health gain but will be vital to alleviate avoidable discomfort. For long-term conditions it would be necessary to hypothesize what the quality of life would be like in the absence of any health care input, which would be difficult to gauge.

Alternatives to QALYs

There are a number of theoretical and ethical concerns over the use of QALYs (Nord, 1992a; Oyebode, 1994). Using QALYs implies that a trade-off exists between length of life and its quality. When given the choice of living for 80 years in poor health or 79 years in full health, many people would probably choose the latter. This is an extreme example, but should illustrate the fact that a trade-off *can* occur. However, there is a debate about how simple such a trade-off is. The QALY theory informs us that 10 years lived with a quality of life rated as 0.5 (on a zero to one scale) is equivalent to 20 years where the quality of life score is 0.25. This is true only if the utility that individuals gain from quality and length of life are independent. If not then QALYs are not an accurate way of measuring benefits (although they may be the best).

Healthy year equivalents

An alternative to QALYs are healthy year equivalents (HYEs), proposed by Mehrez and Gafni (1989). HYEs were developed without the assumptions, contained in QALYs, that utility gained from length and quality of life are independent, or that the utility at one point in time is independent of what has gone on before or will occur in the future. Their proponents argue that HYEs are more in line with economic theory. HYEs are calculated using two stages. First, the standard gamble technique is used to find out at what point an individual is indifferent between N years in a particular state of ill health and an option that could lead to full health or death. Given this probability level, the second stage involves finding out how many years of full health the individual would accept in exchange for taking this option. The poor health/full health exchange means that a *health profile* (the way in which health changes over time) is relevant rather than individual health states at particular times.

This method can be complex. Gafni and Birch (1995) recognize that HYEs are not simple to estimate, but recommend that emphasis should be given to solving the practical difficulties rather than restricting HYEs with assumptions that may invalidate the method. Although there are theoretical strengths of HYEs, these practical difficulties are perhaps the main reason why QALYs, which are simpler to understand, are dominant. Some commentators have demonstrated that HYEs and QALYs, although formulated in different ways, may actually produce the same result (Bleichrodt, 1995).

Saved young life equivalents

QALYs have been criticized by Nord (1992a), who suggests three main problems. First, quality of life measured in numerical terms does not have much meaning. Second, it is assumed that less quality of life is experienced by people who are disabled than for those who are not. This is because the routine use of QALYs often uses weights which are predetermined (as in the health status measures mentioned earlier). Third, there is assumed to be no qualitative difference between health status changes of the same quantitative value. For example, a quality of life score that rises from 0.8 to 1 is considered to be the same as one that increases from 0.2 to 0.4. Nord points out that in reality positive discrimination may be desirable, ie we may prefer to improve the health of the very ill rather than that of the relatively healthy even if the change in health of the former were less than the latter. (This implies that QALYs should be measured on a logarithmic scale rather than a linear one.) He does not reject QALYs, but indicates that they should be limited to providing information on health state changes rather than determining which options should be preferred.

Nord proposes that the time spent in a particular health state should be compared to one particular health outcome, namely saving the life of a young person and restoring them to full health. This is essentially a reworking of the person trade-off approach. In prioritizing treatments, the question that is asked might be 'How many people receiving a hypothetical intervention with a specific outcome, quality of life and experience of treatment, would be equivalent to one saved young life equivalent (SAVE)?' Nord suggests that if the respondent considered that in such circumstances treating 10 people with the hypothetical intervention was equivalent to a SAVE, then the value of this intervention is 0.1 SAVEs. Comparisons across illness groups could be made if different treatments were valued with reference to SAVEs.

The above theory of SAVEs allows outcomes to be measured according to value judgements rather than measured quality-of-life changes, which may not always be appropriate. At first glance it might appear that because a young life saved and restored to full health is the reference category, young lives are considered more valuable than older lives. However, although for many this might be the case, the application of SAVEs would not in theory stop the treatment and outcomes provided to non-young people having a higher value. However, this would mean saying, for example, that 0.5 people treated by the hypothetical intervention were equal to one SAVE. This may be quite a cumbersome procedure. Nevertheless, SAVEs are an interesting concept and could be explored further.

Disability adjusted life years

One of the advantages of QALYs, if they are appropriate, is that they can be aggregated to look at the total benefit arising from an intervention for a particular area – for example, a health authority catchment area. The same is true also for HYEs and SAVEs. The World Health Organization has developed an alternative outcome measure specifically for estimating aggregated burden of illness, known as the disability adjusted life year (DALY). DALYs combine the expected length of life lost due to early mortality with the adjusted number of years lived with a disability. As such they are similar to QALYs, the difference supposedly being in the explicitness with which the assumptions are made (Murray, 1994). However, DALYs have been criticized on theoretical and equity grounds by Anand and Hanson (1995), who claim that they are biased towards those in middle age groups, and because they are discounted they also are biased against people with illness in the future (immediate treatment is given more weight than prevention when benefits are discounted).

Which Outcome Measure Should Be Chosen?

The measure of outcome used in an economic evaluation of a health care intervention will depend on a number of issues. First, many evaluations are dichotomous in nature in that they are primarily a clinical study with an economic component attached. When this happens it will be commonplace for disease-specific measures of outcome to be used, and this may well be appropriate when the question is concerned with choosing between two or more competing interventions for a particular condition. Second, if an evaluation is required to examine the effectiveness of a heath care intervention in comparison with interventions for other illnesses, then a generic measure is necessary. Here outcomes could also be measured in monetary units if the willingness to pay approach is used. Third, if the aim of the evaluation is to determine how the intervention affects the utility of individuals then a generic measure could be used. Fourth, willingness to pay should be employed if societal outcome measures are required. It may be the case that an evaluation requires the use of both generic and disease-specific measures (Fletcher *et al*, 1992; Fletcher, 1995).

Summary

Outcome measurement is the most important and interesting aspect of health economics. An economic evaluation is concerned with measuring changes in the utility that result from health care interventions. While this may appear to be an abstract idea to those directly involved in patient care, it should be recognized that utility simply consists of the benefits produced. As utility includes changes in health condition, it is often appropriate to use a disease-specific measure of health outcome. However, for treatments to be compared across illness groups, generic measures are necessary. The most popular and widespread of these is the QALY, which combines the quality and quantity of life in a single measure. A variety of methods can be employed to calculate the quality component of QALYs. These include direct methods (the standard gamble and the time trade-off being the most suitable) and indirect methods where scores are given to different health states and then used in studies.

A number of problems may exist with QALYs; alternatives exist in the form of HYEs and SAVEs. However, these have not been extensively used. Another alternative is to measure utility in monetary terms using the WTP approach. This has advantages in that all aspects of utility can potentially be incorporated, but there have been difficulties in its application also. The QALY will remain around for some time, but these other methods should be tested further for potential use in decision making.

Important Points for Health Care Decision Makers

- Health gain is a component of utility, gained from health care.
- The process of health care may also generate utility.
- Monetized outcomes using the human capital approach are rarely suitable for measuring outcome.
- Monetized outcomes that employ the WTP method are theoretically the most suitable, but application can be problematic.
- QALYs have been used extensively, and allow treatment for diverse conditions to be compared.
- Problems with QALYs have led some to seek alternatives, such as HYEs and SAVEs, but these need further work and experimentation.

Chapter 5

Types of Economic Evaluation

It was emphasized in Chapter 1 that economic evaluation is crucial if the best use is to be made of scarce resources. Essentially we want either to maximize the outcome achieved from every pound spent on health care, or to minimize the cost of achieving a fixed outcome. A number of different scenarios may occur where economic evaluation is called for, for example:

- An NHS trust may wish to improve its blood donor service and is faced with a choice between increasing the number of mobile units or expanding a hospital based service.
- A health authority may have received more funds from central government than they expected and wish to know whether to spend more on nursing homes or hip replacements.
- Testing is required of a new pharmaceutical product aimed at reducing side effects from cancer treatment.
- A GP practice may have developed a counselling service which they offer to patients, and they wish to know whether this should be replicated elsewhere.

Ideally an economic evaluation should be undertaken of any new health care intervention. However, as Reinhardt (1997) points out,'To date, most decisions concerning treatment methods are still driven by untested or only crudely tested medical theories, as are most of the formularies for pharmaceutical products used in the United States and abroad.' He goes on to suggest that it may be because of the use of complex methods, technical difficulties, or that the assumptions that researchers make are biased. It may also be that health care decision makers are not aware of what economics can offer, other than costing services. In certain circumstances the gains of certain forms of care are felt to be so overwhelming that such an evaluative process is not required. In addition there can be a misguided view that economics cannot morally be used in health care, whereas in reality it may be immoral not to use it. Finally, many health care interventions were developed and established long before health economics had evolved, and these have now become accepted as part of clinical practice. Hopefully the evolution of health economics is now quite advanced, and it is being used more than ever to guide policy at national and local level.

The reasons why an economic evaluation is to take place, the circumstances in which this is to occur and the specific questions that need answering will all determine what sort of evaluation is used and how it is conducted. There are a number of issues surrounding the basic design of any study. For instance, are two or more services being compared? Is the intervention already in place or it is waiting to be implemented? The next section will deal with such issues. This is followed by descriptions of the four main types of economic evaluation: cost-minimization analysis, cost-benefit analysis, cost-effectiveness analysis and cost-utility analysis. The latter three of these are basically ways of synthesizing costs and outcomes which were described in the previous two chapters.

Study Design

If the aim of an economic evaluation is to examine whether an intervention is efficient or not, it is essential that a time-frame is chosen over which to observe costs and the outcome of interest, ie health gain, so that any changes can be detected. By definition, health gain cannot be measured at a single point in time. This is why cost of illness studies generally do not allow questions of efficiency, and hence resource allocation, to be addressed. Cost of illness studies tend to state how many cases of a particular illness exist in a given year and what the associated costs of treatment and productivity loss are. If this was done year on year then changes could be measured, and then broad efficiency indications may arise.

Often two time points are chosen between which costs and outcomes can be measured. For example, in a study of the economic efficiency of community leg ulcer clinics, the percentage of ulcers that were cured within 12 weeks of treatment was observed (Bosanquet *et al*, 1993). The length of time during which a study is performed is crucial, and will be particular to the condition in hand. The effects of coronary bypass grafting should, for example, be measured over a number of years, whereas those associated with different antibiotics for infections could probably be measured over a few days or weeks. Obviously the amount of research money available would determine the length of any study, and a realistic approach for long-term effects is to conduct follow-up studies.

Some studies are conducted *prospectively* and others *retrospectively*. In the former, a hypothesis will be developed and then the service intervention will be observed. The latter examines interventions which have already taken place. Prospective studies are often thought to be superior in that bias concerning the desirability of the hypothesis being confirmed or rejected is less likely to affect the evaluative process.

Types of Sample

When an evaluation is conducted, patients are required for whom costs and outcomes are measured. The method by which patients are sampled influences the validity and impact of the findings.

Randomized-controlled trials

The 'gold standard' method of health care evaluation is to conduct a randomized-controlled trial (RCT). This is where individuals who may receive the intervention in question are randomly allocated either to it or to an alternative form of care. The alternative care is either a standard procedure or no care – for example, a placebo 'drug'. Random allocation means that there will be no systematic bias in the samples in terms of patient characteristics. However, sample sizes need to be sufficiently high for randomization to result in roughly equal subsets of the population such as men or older people. If bias is removed from studies, and the only difference between two samples is that one receives a particular intervention while the other does not, then any differences in outcome are due to the intervention. This ability of RCTs to detect causation is described as *internal validity* (Drummond *et al*, 1997). In some instances it is possible for those collecting data on the patients in an RCT to be 'blind' to which intervention they have received, and occasionally those administering the intervention – particularly if it is medication – can also be 'blind'. Blind and double-blind studies can thus remove researcher and clinician bias from evaluations.

However, there are problems and difficulties associated with RCTs. First, they necessarily preclude a group of people from using the intervention being evaluated. This may be acceptable if the effects of it are unknown, but it may be that the intervention is strongly *felt* to improve health, and stopping someone from benefiting from it on the grounds of randomization can be viewed as immoral. Second, RCTs are often designed to be absent of any factors which may result in the findings being hard to interpret. Many RCTs have age limits on the sample size, and 'problematic' patients are excluded. With evaluations of interventions for schizophrenia it is commonplace for patients who also have a diagnosis of substance abuse not to be included in samples. Reinforcing internal validity in this way is at the expense of the results being used in general settings, ie *external validity* (Drummond *et al*, 1997). Third, an RCT requires a comparison group and this is not always possible, either because of the ethical argument mentioned above, or because of lack of research resources. Fourth, a comparative intervention may be available, but randomizing patients to it is not possible due to its location. For example, one may want to compare ear, nose and throat (ENT) services in Bradford with those in Dorset.

Before and after studies

When and where possible though, RCTs should be used, but given the above potential problems, a number of alternatives do exist. A 'before and after' study can be employed if there is no alternative service with which to compare an intervention. Here patients are used as their own 'controls', ie measures are taken for a period prior to the intervention and for a period following it. For innovative programmes, such evaluations may be a precursor to a more detailed RCT. Some organizations, such as many voluntary groups, may want to know if their service is efficient and this may be the only pragmatic way of ascertaining this. Before and after studies can be advantageous over RCTs in that the evaluation can readily incorporate everyday service characteristics. They do need to be treated with caution, as any changes observed, such as improved quality of life, could be a result of factors other than the intervention.

Matched studies

Matched studies can be used when there is a comparative intervention but randomization cannot take place, such as the above ENT example. Matching requires that samples of patients using each intervention are selected according to factors that could influence outcomes aside from the intervention itself. For example, success in ENT procedures might be influenced by age and, therefore, it would be necessary to have a similar proportion of patients from different age bands in both samples. Matching can also be paired – a female patient aged between 30 and 35 in one sample would only be included if there was a similar patient in the other sample. Matching in reality may take account of a range of factors such as age, gender, ethnicity, marital status and employment. This method of evaluation is sometimes the best option, but it can allow unanticipated biases to creep in and make the validity of any results less secure.

Decision tree analysis

Synthetic studies take place when no patients are sampled, and decision tree analysis is the most widely used approach. A decision tree will generally start off with a choice, such as 'Does the patient receive medication A or medication B?' There may be unique consequences of each option chosen, in terms of other services used and outcomes, and these will have a certain probability of occurring. For complex interventions there may be a number of different choices or consequences that are made throughout the decision tree. The probability of achieving one of a number of final outcomes will be determined by those probability values which preceded it. The probability values used in decision tree analysis are taken from other sources, such as expert opinion or previous studies; and decision trees and other forms of modelling are useful when it is not possible to conduct an evaluation where real situations are observed. They may, though, be prone to manipulation by those desiring a particular outcome, they can be over simple or too complex, and can lack quality (Sheldon, 1996).

Previous studies can also be a valuable source of service use and cost data. It is pointed out by Jefferson and colleagues (1996) that secondary use of this data has not been as widespread as that made of clinical outcome measures because cost methods frequently incorporate particular assumptions. They suggest a number of areas which have to be given attention for this secondary use to happen: the service context in individual studies has to be adequately described; the actual amount of service use should be reported; and differences in technology, currency price levels should be accounted for.

In Chapter 3 the need to explore variations in cost was discussed. In a similar way, where matching takes place, or where two samples are compared which are for some reason unmatched, differences in outcome that are related to patient characteristics, rather than the intervention, also need to be explored.

The following types of economic evaluation all include a cost component, as discussed in Chapter 3. Outcomes are also included, with the exception of the first form of analysis to be outlined, but are measured in different ways. These alternative outcome measures relate to those described in Chapter 4.

Cost-minimization Analysis (CMA)

There is a view that economics is all about cutting costs. However, economic evaluation requires that costs and outcomes be included together. It is tempting to think that if, say, hospital in-patient stays can be reduced, so that costs are cut, then the intervention which achieves that must be efficient. However, hospital in-patient use is not really an economic outcome. If cost were the only criterion on which to base decisions then the preferable option would usually be to do nothing. It can be argued that evaluations with clinical outcomes but no cost considerations are also invalid. Williams (1974) noted that 'Accountants are prone to perpetuate the former fallacy, and medical men the latter, and if the cost-benefit approach did no more than keep these errors in check it would have made a valuable contribution to clearer thinking!' (p 253).

However, there may be different health care interventions where the outcomes are known to be identical. An example of this – GP/midwife or consultant led antenatal care – was given in the preceding chapter. Although the process of care was deemed to be potentially different, there was no difference in outcome if this was measured by the birth of healthy children. (Other outcomes, of course, might differ.) In such scenarios, cost-minimization comparisons can be made as there is no requirement for outcome to be measured. The option which is least expensive *is* the most efficient. It should be apparent that CMAs can only be used in comparing interventions aimed at treating the same condition. An example is given below.

Case study: Cost-minimization analysis of different methods of radiology (Halvorsen and Kristiansen, 1996)

Background: This study took place in a small town of northern Norway. Patients who required radiology for diagnostic tests were referred to a hospital 140 kilometres from the area, while a minority received the service from a local medical centre, where there were no radiologists. Three options were compared: maintaining the current service, referring all patients to the hospital, or teleradiology. The latter enabled diagnostic images to be transferred electronically to the hospital, without the patient having to attend themselves. Patients requiring major examinations were still transferred.

Costs: Three areas of cost were calculated: the radiology equipment, travel expenses and lost production time. Only those equipment costs that would differ between the three services were included. The existing system cost £9 000 more than if the service was all based at the hospital, but the teleradiology service would cost £108 000 more. However, the high cost of teleradiology would be largely offset by decreased patient travel and lost production. Overall, the teleradiology service would cost £6 500 more than the hospital service, and £32 000 more than the existing set-up.

Outcomes: It was assumed that there would be no difference in the health outcomes from these three services, although the quality of service could in theory differ.

Conclusion: The teleradiology option was not cheaper. However, the findings here were influenced by the distance people would otherwise have to travel, and the utilization rates of the equipment. Changing these parameters could alter the findings. The authors did feel that teleradiology might have qualitative and equitable benefits.

Cost-benefit Analysis (CBA)

The term 'cost-benefit analysis' has been used generically for different types of economic evaluation of which 'pure' CBA is only one. CBA uses outcomes measured in monetary units, either by the willingness to pay method or the human capital approach (see Chapter 3). CBA has been particularly used in evaluating environmental or transport projects, rather than health care interventions. This has been largely due to the theoretical problems associated with the human capital approach, and the difficulties of applying willingness to pay questions. With CBA, an intervention is considered to be efficient if the monetized outcomes exceed the costs. Because of this a comparative group is not always necessary. However, policy makers may still approve an intervention even if outcomes do not exceed costs if the deficit is felt worthwhile. The analysis of alternative interventions allows different cost-benefit ratios to be compared, and preferences can thus be made.

If carried out appropriately, CBA can be a powerful tool. Measuring outcomes in terms of money allows health care interventions to be compared with any other activities to which CBA can be applied. CBA should consequently be a valuable form of analysis in comparing different options for public expenditure – for example, hydroelectric dams or liver transplants. In practice, though, it is more probable that different government departments will individually negotiate their budgets with the Treasury, and then conduct evaluations within their specific sphere of operation.

The following case study is a CBA of an evaluation of HIV-antibody testing. It uses a value of life which was estimated according to how much extra people would wish to be paid if employed in jobs that had risks attached. The value of life calculated in this way was US $4.4 million. This was a synthetic evaluation, with figures based on those reported elsewhere in the literature.

Case study: Cost-benefit analysis of routine voluntary testing for HIV-antibodies (La Croix and Russo, 1996)

Background: This study took place in the United States, and the context was that there had been calls for HIV testing of patients in hospitals so that health care workers could take any precautions necessary to minimize their risk of infection. This was obviously a controversial proposal, but one of the more practical arguments against it was the belief that the benefits would not outweigh the costs of testing. However, the authors recognized that benefits would potentially not only accrue to health care workers, but also to the patients themselves and people who they had a sexual relationship with. The test would hypothetically be offered to all patients in a single hospital, but they could refuse it if they wanted.

Costs: These consisted of the materials required to take the necessary blood samples, use of a laboratory, and the time of the health care workers who would conduct the tests and counsel the patients. All patients would be counselled prior to the test and after it if the result was positive. The average cost of such a test was calculated to be US $69.

Outcomes: If health care workers knew of a patient's HIV-positive status then they could take more precautions than usual to reduce the risk of infection. Potentially lives could thus be saved. However, the number would be relatively low due to the limited probability of decreased infection following extra precautions. (The risk of infection with normal precautions, ie when the HIV status was unknown, was already low). The value of a life was estimated to be worth US $4.4 million, but because the probability of infection was so low, this averaged out at US $3.34 per patient tested.

Patients who knew that they were HIV-positive could, with the help of their physician, benefit from prophylactic treatment, which might increase their lifespan. The benefits in terms of increased lifetime, again based on a US $4.4 million value for a full life, were estimated to be US $11 201 per patient tested.

If a patient knew that they were HIV-positive, then they could practise safer sex, and so reduce the risk of their partner being infected. It was not certain of course that this would happen, and the benefit associated with reduced loss of life was estimated at US $5 271 per patient tested.

CBA result: The total benefits that would occur from a single test for HIV status was estimated to be US $16 476 (US $3.34 + US $11 201 + US $5 271). Therefore, the benefit-cost ratio would be 239:1, ie US $16 476 divided by US $69 (the cost of the test). Another way of stating the result would be in terms of the difference between the benefits and costs, ie US $16 476 – US $69 = US $16 407. This overwhelming finding in favour of HIV testing was due to the lives that would potentially be saved among patients and their partners. The costs were greater than the benefits for health care workers, and therefore testing would not be good value if only that outcome measure were used.

The above study did not use the human capital approach to value life, but instead used a value based on observed premiums that workers would demand for working in high risk jobs. However, as with the human capital approach, the assumption is that value of life can be determined by potential earnings. This can be ethically challenged. It also has the same practical problem as the human capital approach in that not everyone would be working anyway even in the absence of illness. The above study, by measuring outcomes in monetary terms, does not allow for other aspects of utility – such as health care worker reassurance, or the negative aspects for patients of testing – to be included in the analysis. However, the scale of the results are of interest, and these criticisms probably do not affect the authors' findings.

The next case study examines the use of the willingness to pay technique in conjunction with a cost-minimization analysis. Although the authors do not describe it as a cost-benefit analysis, by combining willingness to pay with a cost-minimization analysis this is what is effectively achieved.

Case study: Alternative methods of repairing paediatric facial lacerations (Osmond *et al*, 1995)

Background: This Canadian study compared three types of treatment for facial lacerations among children: non-dissolvable stitches, dissolvable stitches and a tissue adhesive. These alternatives were felt to be approximately equal in outcome which is why a CMA would be acceptable. However, because the process of care was different (tissue adhesive was quicker and less painful than dissolvable stitches and, like dissolvable stitches, did not require much after care) willingness to pay was used to gauge the preferences of parents.

Costs: The authors were only interested in comparing the incremental costs of one alternative over another. Therefore, only costs which were different needed to be included. Excluded costs were overheads for the emergency department, registration to be seen, and parental work loss for the first visit to the emergency department. Being equal, these would have a zero incremental cost. Costs that were expected to differ between the interventions were staff and pharmacy inputs, supplies and parental costs subsequent to the first visit. An average wage was used to estimate the value of parental time foregone. Costs were calculated for one patient. Compared to non-dissolvable stitches, dissolvable stitches saved C $37.90 and tissue adhesive C $49.60 (1993 Canadian dollars). Follow-up staff costs and parental time (both of which were required for removal of stitches) pushed up the costs of non-dissolvable stitches. The material costs of dissolvable stitches were far greater than those for tissue adhesive; hence the cost differ-ence between those two.

Outcomes: The clinical outcomes did not differ between the three alter-natives. Thirty parents attending the emergency department with their children for non-laceration treatment were asked for details about their treatment preferences. The reason for asking these parents was that the amount that society would be willing to pay was desired, rather than the amount that parents of current patients were willing to pay. These 'neutral' parents were presented with information about the three treatments and then asked to rank them according to their preferences. They were then asked to state how much they would be prepared to pay for their first and second choices if only the third was generally pro-vided. Information about income and whether their children had ever received such treatment was also collected.

Of the 30 parents, 27 favoured the tissue adhesive and three pre-ferred the dissolvable stitches; 29 parents placed the non-dissolvable stitches in third place. The median amounts that parents would be will-ing to pay for the dissolvable stitches and the tissue adhesive were C $25 and C $40 respectively. These are incremental measures of bene-fit as they were based against the overwhelming third choice which was assumed to be provided anyway. In other words, parents felt that the extra benefits of tissue adhesive over non-dissolvable stitches were worth C $40.

CBA result: This was not described as a CBA, and a cost-benefit ratio was not calculated. An absolute cost-benefit ratio (total monetized benefits divided by cost) is not possible as only costs which differed were included. However, by focusing on the cost difference and the ex-tra amount that parents are willing to pay, an *incremental* cost-benefit ratio is straightforward to calculate. This would simply be the difference in cost divided by the difference in outcome. For tissue adhesive over non-dissolvable stitches this is minus C $49.60 divided by C $40, ie minus C $1.24. Therefore, by spending C $1.24 less, C $1 of benefit is gained. A programme with a negative incremental cost-benefit ratio al-ways means that there is a 'clear-cut' result.

The study above was important in that it calculated incremental societal cost and benefits, by including lost parental time (in other words, productivity losses) and by asking for parents of children not being treated for lacerations to state their willingness to pay.

The study did not use a sample of patients from which to draw cost information, but that was probably acceptable given the relatively homogenous nature of each of the interventions. The authors did perform a sensitivity analysis by altering some cost estimates, and this did not change the results substantially. Lost parental time was measured by earnings which we have seen earlier may be problematic.

Cost-effectiveness Analysis (CEA)

In the previous chapter the use of disease-specific measures was examined. These combined with cost information allow cost-effectiveness analyses to be undertaken within illness groups. This form of evaluation is probably the most widely used, and has to some extent, like CBA, been used to describe all economic evaluations. A view is that that cost-effectiveness is determined by an intervention saving money with no change or no deterioration in outcome. There may be some procedures where outcome is reduced slightly, but huge cost savings are made (Doubilet *et al*, 1986), and this may be clinically acceptable, rendering the intervention 'acceptably' cost-effective.

CEA entails the development of ratios between costs and outcomes. However, although the aim of economic evaluation is to maximize the outcome achieved from money spent, this has to be coupled with value judgements. Doubilet *et al* (1986) provide an example of why the treatment with the lowest cost-effectiveness ratio should not necessarily be chosen.

Case study: Comparison of absolute cost-effectiveness ratios with incremental cost-effectiveness ratios (Doubilet *et al*, 1986)

Treatment A prolongs life for one year and costs US $100. The cost effectiveness ratio is US $100 divided by one, ie US $100. Treatment B prolongs life for five years and costs US $1 000. Its cost-effectiveness ratio is US $1 000 divided by five, ie US $200.

If one were to make decisions according to the size of the cost-effectiveness ratio, then treatment A would be chosen over treatment B. This would, though, appear very harsh. Let us instead examine the *incremental* cost-effectiveness ratio (the difference in cost divided by the difference in outcome). We find that the cost per life year saved from treatment B over treatment A is US $225. We then have to make a value judgement about whether on the basis of this incremental cost-effectiveness ratio treatment B should be chosen over treatment A. In other words, are we prepared to pay US $225 for a one-year gain in life?

The following example of a CEA was based on real data, and examined the costs and outcomes of repeated coronary surgery for recurrent angina. It is interesting that though it is described as a CEA, the focus is on comparing the monetary benefits of regaining work with treatment costs, which would make it a CBA. However, if the numbers of people gaining work are used then a CEA can be generated.

Case study: Cost-effectiveness of repeated coronary surgery for recurrent angina (Dougenis et al, 1992)

Background: Most people who have surgery for coronary artery bypass grafting make a good recovery and return to work. Some people, though, have a recurrence of problems and require a second operation. In this Newcastle-based study, the costs and outcomes of over 40 patients who had repeated surgery were analysed. The average time between initial and subsequent operations was approximately five years.

Costs: These included the cost of the operation itself and related tests, services and medication. GP and out-patient attendances, acute admissions and patient expenses were not costed, but these would have been minor compared to the main intervention when averaged across the sample. The average cost for repeated surgery was £6 289. The total cost for the sample was £308 166.

Effectiveness: This was determined by the ability of the patient to work following the operation. Four groups were defined, and these are shown in Table 5.1 along with the percentage of the sample which they contained before and after surgery. An additional column, calculated from the authors' figures, has been added to show the ratio between the percentages.

Table 5.1 Outcome following repeated coronary surgery

Outcome	Pre-surgery	Post-surgery	Ratio of post- to pre-surgery
No benefit	32.8%	18.2%	0.6%
Benefit but not able to work	28.9%	13.6%	0.5%
Able to work but unemployed	22.4%	36.4%	1.6%
Back to work	16.3%	31.8%	2.0%

Table 5.1 shows that there is a doubling in the probability that a patient will be able to return to work following surgery, and also an increase in the likelihood that the patient would be able to work but remains unemployed. The authors focused, though, on the earnings that could be gained from work, and the tax revenues that would be paid to the government through work. (If gross earnings were used then the inclusion of taxation would actually be double counting, but not if net earnings were used.) It was estimated that the 31.8 per cent of patients in work following the surgery would have earned a total of £69 072, compared to the £32 612 for the 16.3 per cent before the operation. The added financial benefit of the operation was thus £36 460 for the whole sample (excluding taxation).

CEA result: As mentioned above, the outcome that the authors focused on was the earnings received following the operation. Because of this, repeated surgery was not shown to be cost-beneficial – the costs are far higher than the benefits. The gap between benefits and costs was in part influenced by the fact that a number of people able to work remained unemployed. This is a major problem with the human capital approach. However, if the ratio of pre- to post-surgery percentages in work is used as an outcome measure then the result can be viewed differently. In such a case, a health care decision maker would have to decide, for example, whether to spend £6 289 to enable an individual to have double the probability of returning to work following repeated surgery. This is in the absence of other health care benefits, such as improved quality of life, which should also inform the decision making process.

Cost-utility Analysis (CUA)

In Chapter 4, outcome was depicted in terms of the utility gained by individuals. Although disease-specific measures of outcome relate to components of utility they are not comprehensive, and if diverse health care interventions are to be compared then more general measures such as QALYs, HYEs or SAVEs are required. CUA operates in a similar fashion to CEA. For example, the number of QALYs gained are combined with cost information to generate cost-utility ratios or incremental cost-utility ratios.

Case study: QALYs gained from treatment for breathlessness during sleep (Tousignant *et al*, 1994)

Background: Obstructive sleep apnea (breathlessness while asleep) can have a number of effects in individuals, such as memory loss, tiredness during the day, psychological problems and family difficulties. One treatment for the condition is known as *nasal continuous positive airway pressure*, which essentially requires that a special mask be worn while sleeping. This Canadian study sought to calculate the cost utility of this treatment by measuring the QALYs gained from it, and linking these to the care costs for 19 patients. A 'before and after' study design was adopted with no other comparative intervention.

Costs: Only the direct health care costs were calculated. In the study area, the then current (1989) cost of materials necessary for the treatment and an overnight stay in hospital when treatment commenced was C $2 848 per patient. However, there were also estimates of treatment costing C $800 per patient elsewhere in Canada. Life expectancy was assumed to be unaffected by the illness or by its treatment, and the average duration of life after the commencement of treatment was estimated to be 22.3 years. The lifetime costs for all 19 patients were estimated at between C $347 900 and C $1 002 704 depending on the annual cost per patient used.

Outcomes: The treatment was shown to be effective in decreasing breathlessness and many of the symptoms associated with it. The authors used the standard gamble technique to illicit the utility experienced from having the illness prior to intervention, and the utility experienced following it. Patients were offered a hypothetical choice: either remaining in their current health state for a specific number of years (pre-treatment and then post-treatment) or accepting a gamble. The gamble would be a hypothetical treatment that could result in full health (probability = p) or immediate death (probability = 1 minus p). The value of p (which could be between zero and one) was altered until patients were indifferent to remaining in their current health state or accepting the gamble; at this point p was taken to equal utility. The higher the value of p the more likely the gamble would be chosen, as a value of one would mean full health. As p approached zero, meaning that full health would be less likely, the patient would be more prone to accept their current suboptimal health state. As this procedure was carried out for the pre-treatment and post-treatment health states, the change in utility could be observed. It would be expected that the gamble would be more attractive (accepted at lower values of p) for the pre-treatment health state. The gamble should have been less attractive (accepted at higher p values) after treatment. This was indeed the case. None of the 19 patients had lower p values where they were indifferent between the gamble and the current health state after treatment than before it. The average p value before treatment was 0.63, whereas after treatment it was 0.87; therefore the 'utility gain' was 0.24. Without treatment, the remaining (average) 22.3 years of life would be 'worth' 14 years of full health (0.63 multiplied by 22.3). This increases to 19.4 years of full health after treatment (0.87 multiplied by 22.3). Consequently, 5.4 QALYs are gained following treatment.

CUA result: The cost per QALY gained is between C $3 523 and C $9 792, according to the different cost figures (mean cost divided by mean QALY gain). For three individuals the QALY gain was very high. If these are excluded the cost per QALY gain becomes C $18 637.

The study above asked patients to state their pre-treatment utility scores after they had received treatment. This may have led to bias, in that patients who had benefited from a treatment might well feel that the pre-treatment quality of life was worse than they would have stated it to have been in the absence of any treatment.

Whereas the above study took scores from actual patients, the following case study calculates cost utility using a decision tree analysis.

Case study: Cost-utility of surgery versus drug management for medically intractable epilepsy (Langfitt, 1997)

Background: This study lent itself well to cost-utility analysis because of the adverse effect on quality of life that epilepsy can have. The author wanted to know how surgery compared to routine drug treatment in terms of cost and QALYs gained, and in doing this adopted a decision tree analysis. The decision tree started with a hypothetical choice being made between the two alternative treatments. If the surgery option was chosen the patient would first have a form of monitoring to assess their suitability for surgery. If they were not suitable they would receive standard care. If surgery was appropriate the next step would either be the main surgery itself or an intermediate surgical procedure to determine where the focus of seizure was. Following this the patient would either go on to surgery or be referred to routine care. After surgery the patient would have a follow-up phase, along with all those either not initially chosen for surgery or those rejected along the way. Follow-up treatment for all the epileptic patients would depend on treatment outcome; some would require lifetime care, while others could discontinue care if auras and seizures no longer occurred. The probabilities of each of these treatment possibilities and outcomes, and also of death occurring surgery, were taken from the literature or based on other figures.

Costs: Only health care costs were included, and these were based on provider figures. The cost of a patient using a particular service component was multiplied by the probability of this occurring. For example, the procedure to locate the area of seizure cost US $29 286 per person receiving it. The probability of a patient, initially referred for surgery, requiring this was estimated to be 0.32, and therefore the average cost per patient referred was US $29 286 multiplied by 0.32, ie US $9 357. The total lifetime cost of treatment and follow-up was discounted by 5 per cent. Length of life was assumed to be unaffected by outcome, unless death occurred from surgery, and was based on a figure for a healthy 32-year-old woman. The discounted cost per patient referred for surgery was estimated at US $109 362, and the figure for patients cared for with medication was US $84 276. Therefore, the surgery was more expensive than medication management.

Outcomes: The expected length of life was adjusted by quality-of-life figures published elsewhere. The number of lifetime QALYs were discounted (assuming people would want a QALY sooner rather than later). The surgical intervention was estimated to yield 12.12 QALYs and the drug management option 10.51. Therefore, the surgery was more effective than medication management.

CUA result: Because the surgical intervention had better outcomes but higher costs, it did not have a clear advantage over medication management. The incremental cost-utility analysis (difference in costs divided by the difference in outcome) was equal to US $15 581, ie the cost of achieving each extra QALY that would occur if the surgical intervention was chosen. The costs and QALY gains were altered within a defined range for a sensitivity analysis. The incremental cost-utility ratio of surgery over medication was quite sensitive to these changes, but remained positive (higher costs and better outcomes) for most of them. However, the surgical intervention could be seen as 'dominant', meaning that the costs were less and the outcomes better, for some changes in parameters. For instance, if a zero discount rate was used then the medication management costs were higher, because they were predominantly in the future, and discounting reduces the present value of future costs unless a zero rate is used. Surgery entails proportionally more initial costs, and so benefits from a zero discount rate.

Obviously a study such as the one described above is going to be heavily influenced by the probabilities used in the decision tree analysis, and the predetermined quality-of-life scores for the different treatment outcomes. However, the use of sensitivity analyses allowed a number of parameters to be altered, and the overall results were fairly robust to these changes. One controversial aspect concerns the discounting of QALYs. The consensus appears to be that this should not happen as a QALY already takes into account time in the form of length of life.

Summary

This chapter has discussed different methods of economic evaluation. The design of an evaluation will depend largely on the circumstances in which it has arisen. The practicalities of how it should be conducted will be determined by sample availability and also ethical considerations. The four main types of evaluation (CMA, CBA, CEA and CUA) all measure costs in monetary units, but differ in their outcome measures. If evaluations are concerned with comparing different interventions for the same condition, then CEA is suitable. CBA (using WTP) and CUA are appropriate for evaluating within and across diseases categories. In my opinion, the WTP method has definite theoretical advantages over CUA. However, difficulties in its application suggest that CUA is likely to be dominant.

Important Points for Health Care Decision Makers

- RCTs can be the 'gold standard' of economic evaluation, but also have limitations.
- Alternatives are single or matched samples.
- Synthetic evaluations are conducted without samples being directly observed.
- The main types of evaluation (CMA, CBA, CEA and CUA) differ in the way outcome is measured.
- Incremental cost-outcome ratios are generally more useful than absolute cost-outcome ratios.

Chapter 6

Rationing, Evidence-Based Medicine and Prioritization

The concept of 'rationing' health care has proved to be immensely controversial in recent years. In the UK, governments and oppositions have gone on record to stress that they do not, or will not, engage in such an activity. Why does rationing conjure up such adverse reactions? There is clearly an emotive attachment to the term itself, as it brings forth feelings of hardship and austerity. Also the very idea that health provision should be limited, or even curtailed, to people who may undeniably require it is distasteful. However, rationing may be inevitable, if we accept the assumption that health care resources are finite and do not match the demands that are placed on them.

A key point that this book attempts to get across is that scarce resources, and in this case therefore rationing, should not always be considered too negatively. If the problem is reworded to be one of choosing where *extra* health care spending can be allocated, then it is not a choice between who gains and who loses, but rather who gains and who, at the particular moment in time, does not. It can be that there are no losers, only gainers – but not all can gain simultaneously. Rationing during wartime is very different, as consumption of goods does fall and most do lose out. However, if increased expenditure benefits some and not others then there are increasing relative differences, which is a cause for concern that has to be addressed.

This view of inevitable rationing is not universally held, however. Light (1997) has argued that countries like Germany and Holland have a more extensively funded health care system than the UK, and as a result do not have the same problems regarding waiting lists. This is clearly the case up to a point. If health care funding is relatively low, then an increase in funding will meet more needs. But the point is that it will not meet *all* needs. Therefore, the requirement for rationing can be lessened, but it cannot be eliminated altogether. If health care needs are not infinite then there is a case against the inevitability of rationing. This, however, would require that all people were in a state of full health, which is evidently a long way off. It is, though, the case that not all people seek optimum health. For example, there can be a reluctance to make use of dental and optical care, even after the influence of pricing has been taken into account. Light (1997) correctly points out that there is much waste in the health care system and adverse vested interests. If these could be eliminated then rationing could further be delayed. In addition he points out that rationing, as often practised, is inequitable with private patients given preferential or more immediate treatment than non-private patients.

If rationing is to occur, it can do so in two main ways. First, rationing can be implicit. This essentially means that there is an imperfect flow of information among those engaging in the health care process (purchasers, providers and patients). Second, explicit rationing can take place where decisions are made in the open, informed by the best available information. The desire for 'best available information', to enable the efficient allocation of health care resources, was the main reason for the emergence of the evidence-based medicine movement.

Evidence-based Medicine (EBM)

EBM emerged as a discipline largely during the 1990s. It is defined by Sackett *et al* (1996) as 'the conscientious, explicit, and judicious use of current best evidence in making decisions about the care of individual patients' (p 71). There is nothing particularly new about using evidence in medicine, and there should be no doubt that the vast majority of clinicians and nurses have treated patients to the best of their ability, utilizing the evidence generated from their own practice and that of their peers. However, EBM as a concept has led to the integration of evidence and clinical judgement becoming much more explicit.

In the first edition of a journal entitled *Evidence Based Medicine*, Sackett and Haynes (1995) identified the following five aspects of the EBM process:

- Health care information needs are turned into questions which can be answered.
- Relevant information is collected in order to answer these questions.
- The evidence revealed from these sources of information is appraised for validity.
- The answers which are given are applied in clinical settings.
- The performance of clinical work is evaluated in the light of it having received EBM input.

There are concerns that what constitutes EBM can be too influential. For example, Polychronis *et al* (1996) argue that there are aspects of medical practice which cannot be evaluated in a standard way, and that EBM should only be used as a tool to aid the application of medicine, without negating the key role played by a clinician's common sense. It is pointed out by Hunter (1996) that EBM, which is grounded in the science of certainty, is located in an area of uncertainty, namely health care. This is true and is the very reason that randomized-controlled trials are conducted in strict conditions which may not always be applicable in reality. Hunter emphasizes that it is the *probability* of treatment having an effect, and its likely *magnitude*, which are important. He is also concerned that EBM detracts from the judgement of doctors, which is essential due to patient diversity, and that the numerical nature of EBM findings are attractive to governments wishing to contain costs. Carr-Hill (1995) adds that 'often, there are no simple answers to apparently simple questions' (p 1468). Proponents of EBM as a discipline believe, though, that there is no conflict between clinical expertise and best available evidence (Sackett *et al*, 1996).

In actual fact, most of those who see themselves as part of the EBM movement, and those who feel that they are resisting its influence, would accept that evidence and medical skill go hand in hand. I would be as reluctant to have a surgeon operate on *me* if he had never read a textbook on anatomy as I would a plumber who had read every surgical book available but had never stepped inside an operating theatre.

Where does health economics fit into EBM? For some, only the effectiveness of medical interventions should be included. However, this inherently misses the point that resources are limited. It should be the efficiency of medicine which is crucial. It is worth repeating that this does not mean choosing the least costly way of doing something, but examining the relationship between costs and outcomes. Indeed it does not even mean always choosing options which provide the most attractive cost-outcome ratios – this is the point that was made regarding incremental cost-effectiveness ratios in Chapter 5, and will be expounded further in this chapter. If efficiency is crucial in guiding health care choices that are made, then health economics should be an essential component of EBM. It has been pointed out by Clancy and Kamerow (1996) that EBM and cost-effectiveness can cause different conclusions to be made concerning the same problem. They describe cost-effectiveness as a way of allowing planners to identify money spent ineffectively, whereas EBM is of use to clinicians wanting to provide the best care. However, this dichotomy should happen only if EMB is devoid of economic input, or if cost-effectiveness analysis is not constrained by value judgements.

What do we do with the myriad pieces of information generated by evaluative studies, some of which will incorporate an economic component? First of all we need to identify them for the task in hand. A number of ways have been developed in order to do just this, with the most notable being the systematic review. For many years medical journals have included reviews of particular topics, and these have enabled evidence to be collated and aggregated to provide a more definitive answer to a particular question. However, there have been concerns that the studies included in reviews have been collected in a sometimes *ad hoc* way, and the quality and type of study have often lacked consistency. In addition it may be that a literature search is incomplete due to limitations in search programmes, and the fact that studies with negative or inconclusive findings may not be submitted, or accepted, for publication. Therefore, there are a number of biases which may enter into reviews and these may weaken any conclusions.

Systematic reviews are not immune to the above difficulties, but they are conducted in a logical and comprehensive manner. There is generally a qualitative hierarchy of evidence from randomized-controlled trials (RCTs), followed by studies with matched samples, to descriptive reports. The latter are not worse than RCTs, and may add knowledge that RCTs cannot, but they do not allow the effects of an intervention to be definitively identified. A volume clearly describing the process of systematic reviews has been compiled by Chalmers and Altman (1995).

EBM can be applied in different ways according to what 'business' we are in. Clinicians wanting to treat a patient in an effective and efficient way may find the results of a systematic review valuable. Health care planners on the other hand may need to look at a whole range of conditions and treatments in order to prioritize them, which is a consequence of limited resources and therefore the need to ration. It is to the subject of prioritization that we now turn.

Prioritization

That health care resources be prioritized is the logical consequence of the need for rationing and the availability of evidence-based medicine. These three are inextricably linked. If rationing is not required then the other two concepts will invariably not emerge (even though they should – abundance is not an excuse for inefficiency). If evidence-based medicine is not established then the prioritization exercise will be uninformed and could make matters worse. If prioritization does not occur then it is a waste of time talking about the need for rationing and developing evidence-based medicine.

The practice of prioritization

Prioritization is an essential component of health care provision, and it is imperative that it be conducted openly and ethically. If this does not happen then suboptimal methods of rationing may occur (Ryynänen *et al*, 1996). Prioritization can take place vertically (within condition groups) or horizontally (across treatment groups), with the latter entailing the making of more difficult decisions which should involve a range of views (Cochrane *et al*, 1991).

The most famous, and infamous, example of prioritization in action was the Oregon experiment which caused national and international interest. This occurred because of spiralling health care costs (in common with the United States generally) leading to demand for constraint and the desire on the part of the State for adequate healthcare to be provided to its population. A useful summary of the aims of the exercise, which was approved by the Oregon state legislature in 1989, are provided by Bodenheimer (1997) and Blumstein (1997).

Two main issues influenced what happened in Oregon. First, there was a desire to increase coverage by the public (Medicaid) insurance scheme, aimed at those on low incomes. Second, the safeguarding of life-saving treatments was considered essential. This second consideration was in large part a consequence of the tragedy of a young boy called Coby Howard, who died of leukaemia due to the lack of a bone marrow transplant, which was not included in Oregon's Medicaid coverage.

If Medicaid coverage was to be increased to more people then clearly something would have to 'give'. Bodenheimer points out that it was not feasible to reduce the amount of money that doctors received for care provided. Therefore, the only option was to reduce the number of services covered, while maintaining those that were most essential. A list of condition and treatment pairs was prioritized by professionals, members of the community and consumer organizations according to outcome, cost-effectiveness and how many people would benefit. Seventeen condition categories were initially prioritized and then, within these treatments, were ranked. The ranking could subsequently be altered by 'hand' by the prioritization team. Treatments which cured fatal conditions and enabled the return of full health were given the highest ranking, followed by maternity care, treatment for fatal conditions without full health returning, and finally treatments with no or little improvements in health. Around 700 condition and treatment pairs were ranked, and those below number 587 were excluded from the proposed coverage. The list was initially rejected by the federal government.

A revised version where most of the rankings were pretty much the same was accepted. However, the criteria determining how the services were prioritized in the final list were limited to the probability of avoiding death, the cost of avoiding death, and the probability of achieving a health state without symptoms. This latter criterion was also dropped on the grounds that it might discriminate against those who required services but would not return to a symptom-free situation. Therefore, the final list was basically determined by the probability and cost of avoiding death. Blumstein felt that the overriding consideration in determining priorities was that based on medical opinion. In the list rejected by the federal government, net health benefits (valued by members of the public via a telephone survey) were among the factors on which rankings were based, but this was dropped, thereby removing community views about health care outcomes.

There was an earlier list which caused much controversy. This prioritized health care according to cost-utility ratios (although the term 'cost-effectiveness' has confusingly been used in much of the literature reporting the Oregon experiment). Treatments were assessed in terms of their costs, the outcomes that would occur, and the duration of outcome. Eddy (1991) provides a worked example of the cost-utility of treatment for appendicitis, as used in the Oregon experiment (see box).

Such an exercise as the one outlined in the box was conducted for all the treatments initially considered for prioritization in Oregon. The higher the cost per year of full health, the lower down the list would be the treatment. However, the exercise was seen to have failed, which is why the watered-down version was adopted.

The Oregon experiment revealed some bizarre rankings, and it

A patient receiving an appendectomy would face one of four outcomes, and for each of these there was a weight attached to reflect quality of life. These are shown in Table 6.1.

Table 6.1 Appendectomy and quality of life

Outcome	Probability	Quality of life
complete cure	0.97	1.00
survival with abdominal pain	0.01	0.75
survival with other symptoms	0.01	0.63
death	0.01	0.00

If no appendectomy was performed, the probability of death was 0.99 (quality of life of zero), and of full health it was 0.01 (quality of life of 1). The length of life after an appendectomy was assumed to be 48 years, according to the median age of patients. The expected quality of life after an appendectomy is equal to the sum of the products of the probability of being in each particular health state and its associated quality of life, ie (0.97 multiplied by 1) plus (0.01 multiplied by 0.75) plus (0.01 multiplied by 0.63) plus (0.01 multiplied by 0.00) which comes to 0.98. The expected quality of life if a patient with appendicitis does not receive treatment is calculated in the same way: (0.99 multiplied by 0) plus (0.01 multiplied by 1) equalling 0.01. The net benefit from treatment is simply the difference between these two (0.98 minus 0.01), ie 0.97.

The average length of life remaining (48 years) is adjusted by the net benefit (0.97) to calculate the outcome from the treatment (47 years of full health). This is based on the assumption that the benefit of an appendectomy lasts for the rest of one's life. The cost of appendectomy (then US $5 744) divided by this outcome reveals the cost per year of full health (or cost per QALY) gained following treatment. In this case the figure was US $122.

is this which has been at the forefront of criticisms against it. An example provided by Hadorn (1991) shows that tooth capping had a cost per year of full health of US $118 (US $38 for the intervention divided by a net benefit of 0.08 lasting an assumed four years). Tooth capping therefore had a higher ranking than appendectomy, which to most people would be an unacceptable finding. If we *only* consider absolute cost-utility ratios then tooth capping *is* more efficient than appendectomies, and this is probably true if it is compared to other life-saving interventions which by their very nature will often be expensive. Hadorn describes this as an example of cost-effectiveness analysis conflicting with 'the rule of rescue' which means that if life can be preserved it should be, even if apparently this is less efficient than improving quality of life in a cheap and limited way. He claims that cost-effectiveness analysis will inherently prioritize without consideration of the 'rule of rescue', but that it can still be used in drawing a cut-off line on a list of services prioritized in some other way.

In response to these criticisms, Eddy (1991) suggests that economic analysis was not inappropriate, but did not work for two main reasons. First the interpretation of rankings was misguided. The choice should not be about comparing one patient receiving a particular service with another patient receiving a different service but, say, 10 patients receiving one service with 20 patients receiving another. He uses the example of dental caps and surgery for ectopic surgery, where 105 patients can be treated with the former for every one treated with the latter. This appears to make sense in real situations where planning services may involve estimating the volume of people requiring them. However, in a hypothetical situation where equal numbers required each treatment, the ranking could still produce unpopular conclusions.

The second response made by Eddy is that there was inaccuracy in the way in which costs and outcomes were calculated, and this could lead to problems with the ranking. Many services were given the same cost of US $98.51, which was obviously an average used in the absence of more accurate figures. Outcome measurements may have been too broad and insensitive. He gives an example of 55 different types of biopsy having the same net benefit. If costs and outcomes were more accurately calculated then the rankings would inevitably be different. However, there is no evidence that these would have been more palatable. Indeed there is no reason why they should be because, as Eddy rightly points out, cost-effectiveness analysis is neutral.

Oregon was a failed experiment in the application of economic evaluation to prioritization, and the final Oregon health plan was far removed from rankings determined by cost-effectiveness or any other such ratios. The above discussion has suggested some practical problems which may have caused this failure. Oregon was an attempt by one body to attach cost-utility ratios to different interventions, but other 'league tables' have been constructed by assembling the cost-utility ratios from individual studies conducted in specific settings and at different times. Mason and colleagues (1993) identify the following sources of potential difficulty with such league tables:

- Year of study origin: Technological change will alter the costs of services, and inflating them to a common year may not be enough.
- Discount rates used: Some studies discount costs and benefits, others just costs, and others neither. Different rates of discount used will make comparisons problematic.
- Cost calculations: Often only direct health care costs are included. However, some interventions will include costs accruing to other agencies, and patients and their families.
- Comparative interventions: Cost-utility can be measured against doing nothing (which may not have zero costs and outcomes) or an existing standard treatment.
- Setting of study: Comparison of evaluations conducted in different countries will entail use of relevant exchange rates. More fundamental is the fact that clinical practices may well be divergent.

Another source of possible difficulty can be due to trial design. The previous chapter discussed randomized-controlled trials, and pointed out that these are often conducted in experimental settings and might not be replicated. Mason *et al* propose three questions that should be asked by those interested in the findings contained in league tables:

- Can the result be replicated?
- Are the comparisons relevant to my situation?
- Are the costs similar to those in my organization?

They conclude that 'Cost effectiveness estimates should not be used in a mechanistic fashion; at best they provide a useful aid for decision makers' (p 572).

A different critique of what happened in Oregon is presented by Blumstein (1997), who stresses that cost-effectiveness analysis is best suited to situations where 'there is (1) a unitary decision maker (2) allocating a pool of funds (3) in a way that affects all collectively (4) to achieve a defined goal set by a decision maker' (p 549). He argues that unitary decision making regarding which health care services to provide is not feasible, as the population requiring health care provision will have individualistic needs, divergent levels of benefit and different preferences. He contrasts this with other areas of public intervention, such as pollution control, where these needs, benefits and preferences show more similarity across the population. Therefore, economic evaluation at the level of developing health service priorities may not be appropriate. He does, though, suggest that it could be used at a macro-level in determining how much in total to spend on health care, as health care in general does potentially benefit all of society. By suggesting that differences in needs, benefits and preferences lead to such prioritization difficulties, the implication might be that the external benefits a person gains from someone else receiving treatment (for example, the gain that a man gets from women being screened for cervical cancer) are less than the vested interest that an individual has from their own health situation and requirements. This may be true for some individuals but not for others, and as such there will be still be much diversity of preferences.

Economic evaluation is not as problematic as Hadorn suggests, nor is it as appropriate in an Oregon-type situation as felt by Eddy. It is essential in determining service efficiency, and is valuable in informing its prioritization. However, it must be coupled with the capacity for value judgements to be made. Hunter (1996) makes a crucial point when he states that 'If rationing, or priority setting, is treated as a technical problem to be solved through the application

99

of EBM then it will not lead to open, public discussion about what are, at their core, value-based decisions' (p 7).

The Oregon experiment essentially used the QALY concept, but a QALY is the same for someone at the beginning of life or near its end, and for someone who has just become ill or who is close to recovery. Therefore, the cost per QALY can only be effectively used for prioritization if we wish to allocate health care resources equally, which most of us do not. We would rather operate positive discrimination to those who we feel are in most need of health care, sometimes even if their hope of recovery is slight. If such values can be incorporated into the measure of benefit used in QALYs then prioritization may be aided, but this would not be straightforward and other options do exist.

Alternative methods of prioritizing to the original Oregon model

The alternative to using cost-utility analysis in Oregon that was actually chosen has been described above. Condition and treatment pairs were ranked according to the probability and cost of avoiding death. Neglecting to examine other outcomes in otherwise fatal conditions is a very basic prioritization exercise among a defined group of conditions. This is not an appropriate way of allocating resources, because if two condition and treatment pairs rank equally in terms of probability of death avoidance, the least expensive one will be preferred. What though if other factors, encompassed in quality of life, are greatly improved by the service that is not preferred? Some may say that life preservation is all important, and they may be right, but should quality of life be ignored all together?

Assuming that costs and outcome were correctly calculated, a relatively simple improvement that could be made to the Oregon prioritization would be to focus on the incremental cost-utility ratio of one service over another (as shown in the previous chapter). If we look again at the case of appendectomy against tooth capping we find that the incremental cost-utility ratio is US $122 per QALY (difference in costs divided by the difference in outcome). A value judgement then has to be made as to whether we are prepared to pay this amount to secure the health of a patient with appendicitis, over and above the cost paid for a full year's health for someone who requires tooth capping.

In the UK, two opposing views have been put forward as to whether the government should define services which are to be provided by the NHS or not. According to New (1997), health services should be provided if three criteria are met. First the treatment, or condition for which the treatment is aimed, is of fundamental importance. Second, there is an imbalance of information. Third, there is uncertainty surrounding health states. New argues that some services, such as cosmetic surgery, are simply not important enough to be provided by the NHS. The service list should be drawn up without regard for cost-effectiveness or even effectiveness, on the basis of establishing what the NHS should be doing. Once the list is in place, then rationing can go ahead.

Klein (1997) conversely focuses on the problems associated with developing a preferred list. First, the criteria by which it can be done are complex (cost-effectiveness, rule of rescue, physician judgement, community views etc). Second, application of a core list can be practically difficult because 'Inevitably attempts at defining a package of care stub their toes against the rock of patient heterogeneity' (p 507). This was the view held also by Blumstein in his critique of a unitary body making micro-level decisions. Third, if the focus is on which services should be excluded, more sophisticated aspects of rationing may be neglected. For instance it may be that for some patients, decreased staff time or less expensive materials used in interventions are acceptable. This though could have ethical problems, and perhaps even greater ones than if a particular treatment is withheld from all. Finally, Klein points out that even if a set list were created, it would in practice differ from area to area, and equity of access would not necessarily occur.

Community value judgements

There is a view that economic evaluations should incorporate societal costs and benefits rather than just focus on those pertaining to the health care sector and to patients. While the idea of societal costs is fairly well accepted, if not practised, benefits that accrue to society are rarely considered. This is understandable in that a patient who is ill is the main cause for concern rather than those who are not. However, when it comes to prioritizing health care expenditure there is more of a case for taking a broad view of benefits. Anyone can potentially become ill and as such health care services are relevant to all, even those not currently requiring them. To take this one step further, there are grounds for not only prioritizing health care services for the benefit of all of society, but actually letting society do the prioritizing.

One approach to establishing societal health care priorities is to use the willingness to pay (WTP) approach described in Chapter 4. There, the focus was on WTP acting as a measure of utility that patients experienced from a given health care state. However, this can be expanded from the level of evaluation of individual services to the allocation of health funds. If a community's WTP for specific conditions to be treated was revealed, then this could form the basis for conducting economic evaluations of services to treat these conditions. For example, it might be that the residents of a health authority catchment area were willing to pay more taxes for treatment of childhood cancer than for any other condition. If this were the case then the cost-utility or cost-effectiveness of alternative ways of treating childhood cancer could be identified. This process would synthesize the value judgements (including the 'rule of rescue') of individuals regarding which conditions were most important to treat, with the science of economic evaluation to establish the most efficient way of providing treatment.

Case study: Willingness to pay for helicopters, heart surgery and hip replacements

Recognizing that WTP was a potential vehicle for prioritizing health care expenditure, Olsen and Donaldson (1998) sought to see whether this would work in practice. They viewed WTP as more appropriate than QALYs, because the former could include any aspect of an individual's utility function, and was therefore less restrictive than QALYs which were designed to specifically measure quality and duration of life. The study took place in Finland, and it involved asking residents to state how much they would be hypothetically willing to pay for three types of service: a helicopter ambulance, an increase in the number of heart operations, and an increase in the number of hip replacements. These were all actual services provided, and therefore the study was not unrealistic. The services were chosen partly due to their diverse characteristics: the helicopter ambulance was emotionally attractive and would appeal to the 'rule of rescue', heart operations were potentially life-extending, and hip replacements had quality-of-life consequences. The cost of the three options was approximately the same.

Payment for the three services was to be in the form of earmarked taxation, which is appropriate given a publicly funded health care system. People were interviewed and asked to circle a number among a range indicating their maximum WTP. If they were against paying extra taxes, then they were asked to state how much they would be willing to pay by donation or insurance premium. Responses were received from 147 individuals. The mean maximum amounts that they were willing to pay were 316 kroner for the helicopter, 306 kroner for the increase in heart operations, and 232 kroner for the increase in hip replacements. The WTP for the increase in hip replacements was significantly lower than for the two other options. Characteristics of respondents were analysed to see if they had any impact on the WTP amounts stated, and on the relative WTP (for example, the WTP for helicopters divided by the WTP for all three combined).

The ordering of the three options according to stated WTP (helicopter, heart operations, hip replacements), is in contrast to the number of QALYs gained from them which were in completely the opposite direction, as were the cost per QALYs (the highest ranking being for the lowest cost per QALY). This supports the view of Hadorn (1991) that the 'rule of rescue' can conflict with cost-utility analysis. However, it also encouraging to health economists that they have a potential answer in the form of WTP. The authors suggest that that WTP and QALYs work in different ways because the worth of a QALY depends on the circumstances in which it is generated, in particular a QALY associated with a life-saving intervention is worth more than a QALY associated with a technique designed mainly to improve quality of life, even if numerically they are the same.

In the above WTP study the authors seem to suggest that WTP be used to weight QALYs, but it is not clear that it is actually necessary to do this. If WTP produces more reasonable valuations of interventions, why not just use it in the form of a cost-benefit analysis (cost of the services divided by the WTP estimated benefit)? If the WTP technique were used to prioritize broad service categories, then economic evaluation would be suitable to choose specific interventions *within* each category. This in effect would be a form of weighting process.

An alternative method, coincidentally also from Finland, of prioritizing health care services according to community preferences has been proposed (Ryynänen *et al*, 1996). A study was carried out where individuals were presented with a random series of paired scenarios, defined by varying ethical factors (age, income, disease severity, disease prognosis, social status, treatment cost, and whether the cause of the disease was self-inflicted or not). Three factors were included in each scenario, and the respondents were asked to choose between each pair. A statistical analysis was conducted which revealed that treatment for children and patients with severe diseases were preferred, while treatments for older people, those with less severe diseases, or those with self-inflicted diseases were favoured less.

Are such community valuations of disease groups and treatments to be endorsed? In essence it is people who are being ranked, and this might appear to be abhorrent. On the other hand, the 'rule of rescue' would suggest that such prioritizing is immensely altruistic. What though if the priorities made by members of the community are adversely influenced by the media, or by feelings of prejudice? In the study mentioned above, care for older people was given less value than that for children. Is this right or wrong? Health economics can help, particularly via WTP, to facilitate priority-generation. It is not well placed to judge the ethics of it.

Summary

This chapter started off by discussing the idea of rationing, and the consequential concepts of evidence-based medicine and prioritization. Even if health care resources were plentiful due to either adequate expenditure or limited needs, there would still be a requirement to generate information about efficiency and to prioritize services. The use we make of resources is of utmost importance when these are limited, but reducing the limitation should not allow us to be wasteful. Acceptance of inefficient services would curb innovations and medical advancement.

Two methods were tried in Oregon. Initially economic evaluation was utilized to prioritize services. Subsequently, a preferred list which was largely developed according to value judgements was drawn up. These two were effectively seen as alternatives, whereas they perhaps should have been portrayed as complementary ideas. Why not have a preferred list of conditions for which treatment is desired, and then use economic evaluation to choose the most efficient service within that disease grouping?

Willingness to pay has not been used to any great extent in determining community values of different health care interventions. This may reveal a distrust of community opinions, but it is more likely that questions in WTP analyses can be misunderstood. (Respondents may feel they are being asked to pay; policy makers may see it as an opportunity to charge.) However, by posing questions in the form of increased taxation these problems may be overcome. Just because an intervention is valued by the public does not mean that it is technically efficient and, therefore, WTP is perhaps more suitable to broad areas, with cost-utility analysis being used to choose specific services within these areas.

Prioritizing health care spending, as with any other activity which entails using scarce resources, is not only inevitable but also ethically appropriate. However, prioritization carried out using the wrong tools and methods can have an adverse effect.

Important Points For Health Care Decision Makers

- Rationing is seen by many as inevitable, because of limited resources and high demands.
- Evidence-based medicine can inform the rationing process, but

has to be used in conjunction with clinical expertise on a patient-by-patient basis.

- Prioritization is a consequence of rationing and EBM.
- Ranking of interventions in Oregon according to cost-utility ratios did not work due to technical difficulties, but more importantly because cost-utility does not always agree with the 'rule of rescue'.
- An alternative is to use WTP to elicit community preferences for broad treatment options.

Chapter 7

Assessing and Using Economic Evaluations

The aim of this chapter is to provide a guide for health care decision makers who are considering using health economics to evaluate and plan service provision. A number of steps are proposed which should facilitate this process. As there is now an abundance of articles, journal papers, book chapters and reports which describe the economic evaluation of health care interventions, it is essential that these be assessed appropriately. Often they will have been developed with specific questions in mind which might not be particularly relevant in other circumstances. In some cases the methodology employed may have been deficient, leading to dubious conclusions being made. However, a number of 'checklists' have emerged over the years and these will be summarized as an aid to sifting through the evidence which is out there.

Questions that a Health Care Decision Maker Should Ask

Before embarking on an evaluation, and during the course of it, there are a number of issues which a health care decision maker should consider. In so doing, the purpose of the evaluation will be clarified, and the methodology employed will be appropriate. The questions are:

- What problem is being considered?
- Is the evaluation of an established or a proposed service?
- Do alternative services exist?
- Have previous evaluations been conducted?
- What type of economic evaluation is most appropriate?
- Which costs and outcomes are to be included and how are they to be measured?
- How are the results to be presented and disseminated?
- What impact will the evaluation have?

What problem is being considered?

This is the fundamental starting point for health economics input. People who are otherwise busy providing or purchasing health care services do not wake up in the morning and say to themselves, 'I wonder what research I can do today which involves economic evaluation.' Instead, a diligent health care decision maker will be constantly – implicitly or explicitly – seeking to provide services in an effective way and to make the most of the resources they use or organize. This is the essence of economic evaluation. Therefore, the request for health economics input will generally be initiated by a clinical question, for example, 'Am I providing breast cancer screening efficiently?' or 'Are patients with anxiety best seen by a counsellor or a general practitioner?'

Once a specific question has been defined, then the relevance of health economics in answering it can be weighed up. In most situations it will be relevant. Health economics is obviously concerned with the resource implications of different ways of organizing services. However, it has been shown in Chapter 4 that health economists are also interested in measuring the outcomes of health care programmes. Economics is about inputs and outputs, ie costs and outcomes. If it is decided that health economics is called for, a number of further questions have to be asked.

Is the evaluation of an established or a proposed service?

Many services will already be in operation, but may never have been formally evaluated. This is actually true of many interventions that do take place, and even more have never included an economic component as part of an evaluation. This is unlikely with recently developed services, and for some pharmaceutical products there are both political and marketing incentives to provide economic evidence to support their usage. However, individual providers of innovative care may never have been presented with an opportunity of evaluation.

For example, a voluntary organization may have been offering a transport service for elderly people requiring influenza vaccinations in a rural area. This may be a service that should be replicated up and down the country, but who knows for sure unless it is evaluated? It might instead be more efficient for nurses to make home visits. Another example would be of a hospital trust which employs opticians as part of its in-patient service. This might be expensive for the trust, but for the health authority purchasing both in-patient and (for non-fee payers) optical services this may *potentially* be an appropriate way of doing things. The word 'potential' could be replaced by a more definitive term (either negative or positive) if economic evaluation was used. Both replication of services, and assessing their efficiency for internal purposes, can be benefited by health economics.

On the other hand, some services are not in place but are proposed. For example, a health authority may realize that it is not doing an effective job of reducing teenage smoking in its area. What should it do? Options could include distributing information packs via schools, or by mailing them to addresses where teenagers live. Or it could organize school visits by doctors, ex-smokers, or sports personalities. Or it might wish to offer advice whenever a teenager uses other health services. All of these may differ in terms of effects and costs (including the future social costs of smoking). In other cases services may already be in place, but reports of new treatments or procedures might come to the attention of planners who wish to improve their service. Such proposed services either need evaluating elsewhere, or the results generated in other places drawn upon. Some proposed services may not be in place anywhere, and in such circumstances a modelling exercise would be the most feasible option for evaluation.

If a service is already established, then it makes sense for economic evaluation to focus upon what is currently happening. If replication of it is desired, it might be necessary to make such an evaluation more generalizable. The next question to be asked concerns stand-alone versus comparative evaluations.

Do alternative services exist?

If a health care intervention has already been introduced, it will often be in parallel with an existing service. An example would be of a day centre for people with learning difficulties running alongside day activities in a group home. Clearly many people with learning difficulties do not require such residential care, but if the level of day care is a common need it might potentially be more effective and less expensive to combine this aspect of the two services. A comparative evaluation of the different options would inform those making such decisions.

In fact there will frequently be alternative ways of providing health care to the same client group even if only one of these actually does occur. When service evaluation takes place it is important to compare it with the most reasonable alternative. An evaluation of different forms of cancer drug treatment by a hospital should not be compared with innovative unproved regimes. Standard care generally forms the most useful comparator to treatments under evaluation.

Health services will on occasion have no appropriate comparison group. This will be particularly the situation with innovative programmes. If there is no alternative form of care that can serve as a comparator even in a 'synthetic' way (for example, using decision tree analysis), or if research time and money (both also scarce resources) preclude comparative analysis, then the best form of evaluation would be to use the clients receiving the service as their own controls, in the form of a before and after analysis. If no 'before' and 'after' time periods can be defined, the most that can be done is to perform a descriptive study, which could still compare costs and clinical features, but outcomes are not really measurable in this way, other than by measuring outcomes from continued use of a service which is not especially meaningful except that it gives an indication of any trends that occur.

Deciding what comparison service, if any, is to be used in an economic evaluation is actually fundamental to the original question being asked. It is not that informative to determine service efficiency in absolute terms because it is a relative concept (service A is more efficient than service B, but is less efficient than service C). A degree of absolutism can be introduced if we compare service A to doing nothing, and indeed when comparing diverse health care interventions this is the most straightforward way forward; in the construction of QALY league tables the 'do nothing' comparator is common.

Have previous evaluations been conducted?

The next question is concerned with evaluative exercises that have been conducted previously. As stated above, research time and money are not unlimited, and yet there are many existing and proposed services which require evaluating. If we take a societal perspective, as economists try to do, it is no less immoral to squander research resources than it is to spend health care finance in a less than optimal way. A careful examination of research evidence is a vital investment in the evaluative process, and can allow decision makers to focus on other areas that deserve attention. The importance of disseminating and using best available evidence on effectiveness and costs is the substance of evidence-based medicine, as discussed in the previous chapter. There are a number of organizations that are formally engaged in the practice of evidence-based medicine, alternatively known as health technology assessment (HTA). However, these organizations will not have answered every question that is being asked by a local decision maker, and therefore original sources of information should be utilized. Table 7.1 suggests a range of these sources.

While overlapping, the items listed in the box differ in their emphasis and quality. For example, the Cochrane database has a large emphasis on RCTs. These are crucial in establishing the definitive effects of a health care intervention, but they may not be relevant in the situation that caused the health care decision maker to ask their initial question. Computer databases will enable a vast amount of literature to be identified, but skill is required in formulating requests and the coverage of included journals can be substantially below 100 per cent. Many relevant publications will also not be included in the most common databases. Peer-reviewed journals are usually the best source of scientific evidence about an intervention. However, more commercially run publications, which are often not peer-reviewed, are a good source of everyday practice. The optimal solution may be to seek out a variety of information sources, rather than to focus on only one area. Unswerving loyalty to particular types of evaluation can confine the health care decision maker too much.

Table 7.1 Sources of evaluative evidence

Individual systematic reviews
Medical journals
Social care journals
Non-indexed publications
Databases (Cochrane, Medline, Embase etc)
Reports from government, professional and academic bodies
Unpublished information
Personal communications

Therefore, while using previously released evidence is vital, the decision maker should be concerned that it is relevant to their circumstances. Differences in study setting and sample, and design of the trial can lead to different outcomes being experienced. Some differences though may be slight and not that influential, and in any case for some services it will be rare to find evaluations which are totally relevant. As with searches for evidence, application of it should be pragmatic.

Conducting an evaluation when the evidence from other sources has conclusively answered the question one way or another or where the weight of evidence has been found to be significantly in one direction is wasteful. This though does not mean that studies should never be replicated. Because of stringent study conditions, RCTs may need repeating elsewhere. Likewise, loose study conditions for non-randomized trials may also demand replication. In addition, different studies may have revealed diverse results. The decision maker, therefore, needs to make a value judgement concerning the existing evidence, to assess whether or not a new evaluation is required. If no evaluation has taken place before, then it is generally appropriate to conduct one.

It is unfortunate that many evaluations of effectiveness have not included an economic component. In such circumstances it may be necessary to conduct only partial evaluations where economic data are synthetically attached to existing results. Though very much a second best alternative, this option can lead to fairly rapid conclusions being made. This would be more difficult the greater were the number of individual service components to be included, as each of these might potentially vary given any change in the form of service provision. Consequently, synthetically calculated economic data would be most suitable in comparisons of drug treatments for well-defined conditions, rather than for community care services provided to broader client groups. If the health care decision maker realizes that an economic evaluation is required to answer their specific question, then the next question to ask will be to do with the type of evaluation they should conduct.

What type of economic evaluation is most appropriate?

Three main influences will determine the answer to this question. First, it will evidently depend largely on the initial question which has been asked already. Details of the circumstances under which different types of evaluation can be conducted have been dealt with in Chapter 5. There it was suggested that while RCTs are often seen as the gold standard, they are not the only method nor are they in all circumstances the ideal one. Second, the logistics (time, finance, expertise available etc) will have a substantial say in the evaluative process. Third, the purpose for which the answer to the initial question is to be used will be important. For example, if a hospital trust wishes to choose between different ways of treating patients on dialysis, it may want to conduct only a basic non-randomized evaluation. Using clinical expertise, it will know best how to interpret any findings based on the patients using the services. However, if the results are to be used by trusts elsewhere then a study containing many local idiosyncrasies will not be suitable.

For some evaluations it may not be possible to look at people actually using the service. This will be so in the aforementioned situation where a service has only been proposed rather than actually being in place. Also it may be the case that research resources prohibit an extensive study from taking place. In circumstances such as these the usual option is to use a decision tree analysis.

Which costs and outcomes are to be included and how are they to be measured?

Once the study design has been formulated, the next step is to focus on costs and outcomes. The interests that caused the health care decision maker to ask their question will often be the main determining factor here. It has been proposed in earlier chapters that costs and benefits should ideally be examined with reference to a broad perspective. More money spent on the health care sector means less on other areas, and because anyone can potentially become ill we all can benefit in some way from care. However, it is recognized that costs that are borne by the health care sector will frequently be of most interest, and outcomes that are experienced by patients will have prominence. This is understandable – most evaluations of health care interventions take place in the health care sector and are designed to improve people's health. In the light of this what is important is that any restrictions that are placed on cost and outcome inclusions are specifically stated.

Whether costs and outcomes are confined to the health care sector and patients, or whether a societal view is taken, it is important that changes in these parameters are detected. If the health care sector is of prime importance, it is imperative that all relevant health care costs be included, and this should be on the basis of those that can potentially change. Consequently, cost measurement has to be accurate, especially for those services most affected by the intervention. In a similar way, the correct measures of outcome should be measured appropriately. It might be necessary to include different instruments which measure the same factor in order to obtain a degree of reassurance concerning the findings.

In decision tree analysis, costs and outcomes are not measured directly but are estimated and/or collected from other analyses. Also the probabilities associated with each decision tree branch are based on informed assumptions. It is important that the source materials for these estimations be relevant to the study question. Sensitivity analyses can be used to assess the impact of changing such parameters.

Marginal costing is recommended for use in economic evaluations. In Chapter 3 it was stated that long-run marginal costs may be approximated by looking at current average costs. Even though this simplifies matters, it should not detract from the fact that decisions are more often than not made at the margin.

How are results to be presented and disseminated?

The question suggested here is concerned with ways in which results of evaluations are presented and disseminated. Yet again, the question being asked in the first place should direct these considerations. If the purpose of the evaluation is to derive a cost-utility ratio, then essentially only the average cost and outcome figures need to be calculated and reported. This will be especially so in an RCT where patient characteristics are not systematically different according to treatment groups. However, even in RCTs it will be interesting to see what impact differences in characteristics have on outcomes and costs, and it is actually not a difficult task, given some statistical input, to explore results in this way.

It is also helpful to present both results, and details of the study setting and sample, in a way that enables replication and informs practice elsewhere. The ability of a study to be included in a systematic review is also a positive aspect that should be aimed at. These considerations may not be felt to be of much relevance when undertaking an evaluation, but adherence to them can make the

results of a study that much more powerful, and can save future research resources. Following on from this, disseminating evaluative
evidence is important. Often this will be in the form of peer-
reviewed journal papers. Other, often more practically based, publications have broad audiences and would also be a worthwhile vehicle for getting research findings out into the wider world. In
addition, conferences are a good forum for the dissemination of
evaluations that do not always get published.

What impact will the evaluation have?

Before a health care decision maker embarks upon an economic
evaluation, the effects of it should be addressed. Obviously there is
a huge amount of uncertainty here, and it would be unreasonable
to expect an evaluation to be cancelled because of this lack of fore-
knowledge. Some indicators though are available. The impact of
the evaluation will be determined by the question asked, the
answer provided, and the means by which it was arrived at. Some
areas of health care research may be of particular interest, such as
alternatives to in-patient care and improved access to services. The
asking of an obscure question may result in a wonderfully conducted study and clear outcomes, but will probably have next to no
impact. This again brings the appropriateness of some evaluations
into question. The Department of Health in the UK has tackled this
issue and regularly releases calls for research into specific areas.

Although any one study, no matter how relevant and
well-conducted, is unlikely to change the course of medicine, it is
true to say that there is a cumulative effect of research. If many
studies evaluate the same type of intervention and generally reveal the same results, we would expect policy makers to recognize
this, and for practice to change as a result. The whole point of evidence-based medicine is to make results accessible, and this should
reduce the number of evaluations that a specific intervention
needs to undergo. However, it has to be recognized that much
good research either goes unnoticed or is ignored by many, and
this an issue that has to be faced by managers, clinicians and researchers alike. The question of available evaluative evidence has

been briefly discussed already. We now turn to this in some more detail.

How To Spot a Good Evaluation

The main substance of this book has been to describe the various options available to those conducting an economic evaluation. We now turn to a summary of what features of an evaluation should be present in order for them to affect the way in which health care is practised. Over the years a number of 'checklists' have been produced to aid the assessment of evaluations, by journal editors, reviewers, authors and also those wishing to use the findings. Tables 7.2, 7.3 and 7.4 give details of checklists that have been published by Williams (1974), the UK government and pharmaceutical companies, discussed and adapted by Rapier and Hutchinson (1995) and Drummond *et al* (1997). There is much similarity between these lists, and they should be seen as progressive refinements of each other. They are recognized by their advocates to be in a sense idealistic, and not all studies will fulfil them (Drummond *et al*, 1997), nor do all studies, such as those measuring the cost of illness, need to (Rapier and Hutchinson, 1995). At the end of the day, as Rapier and Hutchinson point out, peer review of papers is still essential.

Table 7.2 Checklist for assessing economic evaluations (Williams, 1974)

1. What precisely is the question which the study was trying to answer?
2. What is the question that it has actually answered?
3. What are the assumed objectives of the activity answered?
4. By what measures are these represented?
5. How are they weighted?
6. Do they enable us to tell whether the objectives are being attained?
7. What range of options was considered?
8. What other options might there have been?
9. Were they rejected, or not considered, for good reasons?

10. Would their inclusion have been likely to change the results?
11. Is anyone likely to be affected who has not been considered in the analysis?
12. If so, why are they excluded?
13. Does the notion of cost go wider or deeper than the expenditure of the agency concerned?
14. If not, is it clear that these expenditures cover all the resources used and accurately represent their value if released for other purposes?
15. If so, is the line drawn so as to include all potential beneficiaries and losers, and are resources costed at their value in their best alternative use?
16. Is the differential timing of the items in the streams of benefits and costs suitably taken care of (eg by discounting and, if so, at what rate?)?
17. Where there is uncertainty, or there are known margins of error, is it made clear how sensitive the outcome is to these elements?
18. Are the results, on balance, good enough for the job in hand?
19. Has anyone else done better?

Table 7.3 Checklist for assessing economic evaluations: UK guidelines (in Rapier and Hutchinson, 1995)

1. Was the question being addressed by the study identified?
2. Was the patient population defined?
3. Was the choice of comparator explained?
4. Were the different treatment paths clearly presented?
5. If indirect costs were measured, were they reported separately from the direct costs and benefits to the NHS?
6. Was a recognized type of economic analysis used?
7. Was the reason for choosing this technique explained?
8. Was the cost of additional benefits reported?
9. Was the choice of outcome measures explained?
10. Were all relevant costs identified?
11. Was resource also expressed in physical units?
12. Was discounting clearly reported?
13. Were adequate sensitivity analyses conducted?
14. Were appropriate comparisons made with other studies?

Table 7.4 Checklist for assessing economic evaluations (Drummond *et al*, 1997)

1. Was a well-defined question posed in an answerable form?
2. Was a comprehensive description of the competing alternatives given (ie can you tell who, did what, to whom, where, and how often)?
3. Was there evidence that the programme's effectiveness had been established?
4. Were all the important and relevant costs and consequences for each alternative identified?
5. Were costs and consequences measured accurately in appropriate physical units?
6. Were costs and consequences valued credibly?
7. Were costs and consequences adjusted for differential timing?
8. Was an incremental analysis of costs and consequences of alternatives performed?
9. Was allowance made for uncertainty in the estimates of costs and consequences?
10. Did the presentation and discussion of study results include all issues of concern to users?

The questions posed in the lists in Tables 7.2, 7.3 and 7.4 are certainly of great importance, but they could be off-putting if the only evaluations from which a health care decision maker has to make conclusions fail to provide satisfactory answers to them. Undoubtedly, the impact of such studies can be limited. However, they should not be seen as redundant – often they will have particular qualitative relevance. Decision makers, like those engaged in peer review, must exercise sound value judgement and examine each evaluation they are faced with on its own merits. The guidelines are what they claim to be – guides.

Summary

This chapter has described a series of questions which a health care decision maker should ask when considering to use health economics to evaluate a service. It has been emphasized that it is the initial question that is being asked which will influence the design of the study, the comparisons that are made, the costs and outcomes which are measured, and the way in which the results are reported and used. Evaluations that have already been conducted can usually be found in peer-reviewed medical journals, as well as in commercial practice journals. A series of checklists/guidelines have been developed, which can aid those wanting to learn from evaluations which have already taken place. In all of this, and in fact in health economics generally, it is not so much that every element of an evaluation take place perfectly, but rather that evaluators be explicit about how they have conducted their work, and why the preferred methods were chosen.

Important Points For Health Care Decision Makers

- Prior to embarking on an evaluation, a health care decision maker should be clear about the problem which they are addressing.
- Previous evaluations may have already answered the relevant questions making a new one unnecessary. However, on occasion replication of evaluations is required to confirm findings.
- The type of evaluation and the way in which it is conducted will be determined by the initial question asked, and the circumstances in which it was posed.
- Evidence that is reported in the literature should be utilized, but has to be analysed so that the maximum benefits may be gained from it. To aid this, checklists are available.

Chapter 8

The Future Role of Economics in the Health Arena

The aim of this concluding chapter is to summarize where we have come from in health economics and where we are likely to go. This of course will depend very much on political and organizational changes that are taking place in the health sector, both in the UK and elsewhere. Many of the techniques used in health economics have been developed in the United States, and therefore health policy in that country has indirect consequences on the way in which evaluations are conducted here.

The view was put forward in the introductory chapter that health economics has developed in line with broader shifts in economic thinking. This should not be surprising, as health economics is not theoretically independent of mainstream economics. The emergence of many cost of illness studies can probably be located in a time when concerns about the post-war boom were growing, and health care costs, particularly in the United States, were increasing at a high rate. The fact that such cost-consciousness led to the emergence of tools designed to evaluate health care interventions should not be viewed in a negative way. Few people desire health care expenditure to be unreasonably limited, but overt decision making, albeit as a result of scarcity, is a positive outcome. It has been suggested on a number of occasions

that even if resource scarcity was not a problem, efficient allocation of resources would still be called for. There are many other services which require funding, and many of these actually have
health-improving potential, for example housing, education and
employment training. Poverty is one of the root causes of ill health,
and there is a case for saying that health expenditure is on occasion
dealing with the effects of poverty, which other public expenditure could alleviate.

Current Emphases

Health economists have tended to move away from macro-type
evaluations, where whole disease groups are costed, towards mi-
cro-evaluations of specific interventions. The former type of work
did not actually have much to do with economics, whereas the latter is well grounded in utility theory which is the mainstay of micro
economics. Economists view individuals as utility maximizers, and
it is in the measurement of utility that much work has been and is
focused. Economists are not in conflict with clinicians in this –
health care benefits are a crucial, if not *the* crucial, element of an ill
person's potential utility. The emergence of the QALY is the best
example of how utility measurement has been deployed in the
health field. However, there is an interest in alternatives to QALYs,
such as SAVEs and HYEs, due to the possible inflexibility of the
QALY assumptions. These though have not established themselves in UK practice, as QALYs have.

A more comprehensive approach to measuring utility is to use
willingness to pay (WTP). This also has yet to be used extensively
outside of academic circles, but has much potential. An alternative
which has not been mentioned previously is *conjoint analysis*,
which allows treatment options to be chosen by individuals on the
basis on various attributes they have. This may be more acceptable
than WTP, and the latter can sometimes be deduced from it (Ryan,
1993).

Implications of Policy Change

In the UK the emergence of the internal market and GP fundholders in the early 1990s led to an increased demand for cost and outcome information. A market system can only operate efficiently if such information is available, and this is no less the case for health care, even if there are arguments about whether it should be open to market interactions anyway. The late 1990s has seen proposals to end these two policies in favour of primary-care-based purchasing in general. If consortiums of GPs are to make appropriate decisions as to what should be financed and provided, and in what ways, then the information flow has to increase further. The continuing establishment of evidence-based medicine is a timely aid to this, but it has to incorporate high quality economic information concerning both costs and outcomes. The onus is on managers, clinicians and economists alike in this respect.

Where Now For Health Economics?

In 1987 Culyer, recognizing that UK heath economics tended to concentrate on economic appraisal of particular health care interventions rather than institutional policies such as health care insurance, felt that the future would see more of this focus. This has been the case to a large extent. In the UK, although economists have discussed and analysed the workings of the internal market, we have not reached the situation that exists in the United States where profit making health care providers abound and packages of managed care are sold. This is likely to remain the case for the foreseeable future, for though the current government will aim to change the way in which the NHS works, this is not expected to result in more market mechanisms introduced but rather the opposite. Because evidence-based medicine is probably going to grow in importance, the future that Culyer saw will most probably be realized to a greater extent over the coming decade.

In 1981, Abel-Smith suggested that attention needed to be paid to the *causes* of ill health as well as the treatment of it, and he felt that epidemiological research was therefore vital. The importance of evidence-based medicine has been stressed in this volume, but there is a danger that it can focus efforts on treatment at the expense of prevention, and health economists have yet to enter into the area of illness prevention as extensively as they might.

If it is accepted that economic evaluation is required to allocate resources between alternative interventions, and that this is particularly driven by resource scarcity, then the logical extension of this argument is that health economics should be used extensively in developing countries. Developing countries obviously have even greater limits on spending, and far higher needs, than industrialized nations.

Consequently it is imperative every amount of money spent achieves its maximum potential. However, as with economic evaluation elsewhere, value judgements have to form the framework within which it operates. This means that the focus may be predetermined, and examination of alternative ways of improving survival and eradicating fatal but potentially curable diseases may dominate evaluations. Future health economic evaluations need to recognize areas where the need is greatest.

It is often the complaint of economists that clinicians make decisions without recourse to economic information. This is perhaps less the case now than a decade ago. In 1984 Ludbrook and Mooney recommended three areas for action: 'educational activities; initiatives to persuade, cajole and coerce individuals at least to want to undertake economic appraisal; and practical support to manage the change and to sustain the application of economic appraisal' (p 21).

In the mid-1980s, Spoor et al (1986) noted with concern that health economics was not being taken on board by clinicians, and in 1992 Mooney again emphasized the important role that economics can have in health care decision making, and proposed that clinicians and nurses receive some training in the subject. It is probably the case that health economics has now become more accepted among non-economists, but this is by no mean certain.

This volume has hopefully demonstrated that health economics has a key role to play in health care evaluation. As such, it is also hoped that it will become a resource which health care decision makers can utilize to the benefit of patient care.

Glossary of Abbreviations

CBA Cost-benefit analysis A way of conducting an economic evaluation where costs and outcomes are both measured in monetary units.

CEA Cost-effectiveness analysis An economic evaluation method where costs are measured in monetary units and outcomes are measured in medical units eg reduction in pain.

CMA Cost-minimization analysis A method of economic evaluation where costs are measured in terms of money and outcomes are ignored. This is only suitable when outcomes are known beforehand.

COI Cost of illness This is a means of measuring the overall economic consequences of an illness or disease. Treatment costs are included as are the costs of lost production.

CUA Cost-utility analysis The most recent form of economic evaluation in health care. Here costs are measured in monetary units and outcomes in utility scores (usually proxied by quality of life). Generic utility measurements allow comparisons to be made across medical specialities.

DALY Disability adjusted life year Similar to quality adjusted life years. They have been developed by the World Bank for valuing different health states, and combine quantity of life lost from an illness with the disability experienced during remaining years.

EBM Evidence-based medicine This is the generic term given to the process of implementing health care interventions if the evidence suggests that they are effective.

GDP Gross domestic product The monetary value of the output of the entire domestic economy.

HYE Healthy year equivalent An alternative to quality adjusted life years, which does not assume that quality and length of life are independent. It takes into account changes in health status during the profile of an illness.

NHS National Health Service The institution which provides health care to most of the UK population.

QALY Quality adjusted life year Often cited as the most appropriate way of measuring health outcomes because it allows diverse interventions to be compared. QALYs adjust length of life according to its quality. Ten years lived at a quality of 0.5 on a zero to one scale is equivalent to five QALYs. Quality and quantity of life are deemed to be independent and, therefore, these five QALYs would be equivalent to five QALYs generated by 20 years with a quality score of 0.25.

RCT Randomized-controlled trial A means of comparing two or more interventions. The influence of patient differences is removed by random allocation to these interventions.

SAVE Saved young life equivalent An alternative to QALYs where respondents are asked to state how much the outcome of an intervention is worth in terms of saved young lives.

WTA Willingness to accept This is a way of measuring the value of a health state in monetary units. Respondents are asked to state the hypothetical minimum amount of compensation they would be willing to accept if they were to experience a particular level of ill health or health deterioration.

WTP Willingness to pay Similar to and more popular than willingness to accept, respondents say how much they would hypothetically be willing to pay to experience an improved level of health.

References

Abel-Smith, B (1981) 'Health care in a cold economic climate', *Lancet*, 14 February 1 (8216), pp 373–6.

Allen, C and Beecham, J (1993) 'Costing services: ideals and reality', in *Costing Community Care*, ed A Netten and J Beecham, Ashgate, Aldershot.

Anand, S and Hanson, K (1995) *Disability-Adjusted Life Years: A Critical Review*, Harvard Center for Population and Development Studies, Working Paper Series Number 95.06, Harvard School of Public Health, Cambridge.

Association of the British Pharmaceutical Industry (1965) *The Cost of Mental Care*, Office of Health Economics, London.

Auster R, Leveson, I and Sarachek, D (1969) 'The production of health, an exploratory study', *Journal of Human Resources*, **4** (4), pp 411–36.

Baumol, WJ (1995) *Health Care as a Handicraft Industry: A Look at the Contribution of Relative Productivity Growth to the Ill Health of Health Care Expenditure, and How to Adapt to the Chronic Cost Disease*, Office of Health Economics, London.

Berwick, DM and Weinstein, MC (1985) 'What do patients value? Willingness to pay for ultrasound in normal pregnancy', *Medical Care*, **23** (7), pp 881–93.

Bleichrodt, H (1995) 'QALYs and HYEs: Under what conditions are they equivalent?', *Journal of Health Economics*, **14** (1), pp 17–37.

Blumstein, JF (1997) 'The Oregon experiment: the role of cost-benefit analysis in the allocation of Medicaid funds', *Social Science and Medicine*, **45** (4), pp 545–54.

Bodenheimer, T (1997) 'The Oregon health plan – lessons for the nation. First of two parts', *New England Journal of Medicine*, **337** (9), pp 651–5.

Bosanquet, N *et al* (1993) 'Community leg ulcer clinics: cost-effectiveness', *Health Trends*, **25** (4), pp 146–8.

Brazier, JE *et al* (1992) 'Validating the SF-36 health survey questionnaire: a new outcome measure for primary care', *British Medical Journal*, **305** (6846), pp 160–4.

Carr-Hill, R (1995) 'Welcome? to the brave new world of evidence based medicine', *Social Science and Medicine*, **41** (11), pp 1467–8.

Carr-Hill, RA and Morris, J (1991) 'Current practice in obtaining the "Q" in QALYs: a cautionary note', *British Medical Journal*, **303** (6804), pp 699–701.

Chalmers, I and Altman, DG (1995) *Systematic Reviews*, BMJ, London.

Clancy, CM and Kamerow, DB (1996) 'Evidence-based medicine meets cost-effectiveness analysis', *Journal of the American Medical Association*, **276** (4), pp 329–30.

Cochrane, M *et al* (1991) 'Rationing: at the cutting edge', *British Medical Journal*, **303** (6809), pp 1039–42.

Cooper, BS and Rice, DP (1976) 'The economic cost of illness revisited', *Social Security Bulletin*, **39** (2), pp 21–36.

Croft-Jeffreys, C and Wilkinson, G (1989) 'Estimated costs of neurotic disorder in UK general practice 1985', *Psychological Medicine*, **19** (3), pp 549–58.

Culyer, AJ (1987) 'The future of health economics in the UK', in *Health Economics: Prospects for the Future*, ed G Teeling Smith, Office of Health Economics, London.

Davies, LM and Drummond, MF (1990) 'The economic burden of schizophrenia', *Psychiatric Bulletin*, **14** (9), pp 522–5.

Donaldson, C (1993) *Theory and Practice of Willingness to Pay for Health Care*, Health Economics Research Unit Discussion Paper No 01/93, University of Aberdeen, Aberdeen.

Donaldson, C and Shackley, P (1997) 'Does "process utility" exist? A case study of willingness to pay for laparoscopic cholecystectomy', *Social Science and Medicine*, **44** (5), pp 699–707.

Dor, A, Held, PJ and Pauly, MV (1992) 'The Medicare cost of renal dialysis: Evidence from a statistical cost function', *Medical Care*, **30** (10), pp 879–91.

Doubilet, P, Weinstein, MC and McNeil, BJ (1986) 'Use and misuse of the term "cost effective" in medicine', *New England Journal of Medicine*, **314** (4), pp 253–6.

Dougenis, D, Naik, S and Hedley-Brown, A (1992) 'Is repeated coronary surgery for recurrent angina cost effective?', *European Heart Journal*, **13** (1), pp 9–14.

Drummond, MF (1980) *Principles of Economic Appraisal in Health Care*, Oxford Medical Publications, Oxford.

Drummond, M (1992) 'Cost of illness studies: major headache?', *Pharmaco-Economics*, **2** (1), pp 1–4.

Drummond, MF *et al* (1997) *Methods for the Economic Evaluation of Health Care Programmes*, 3rd edn, Oxford Medical Publications, Oxford.

Dublin, LI and Lotka, AJ (1930) *The Money Value of a Man*, Ronald Press Company, New York.

Dublin, LI and Whitney, J (1920) 'On the costs of tuberculosis', *Quarterly Publication of the American Statistical Association*, **17** (4), pp 441–50.

Dubourg, WR, Jones-Lee, MW and Loomes, G (1994) 'Imprecise preferences and the WTP-WTA disparity', *Journal of Risk and Uncertainty*, **9** (2), pp 115–33.

Eddy, DM (1991) 'Oregon's methods: did cost-effectiveness analysis fail?', *Journal of the American Medical Association*, **266** (15), pp 2135–41.

Essink-Bot, M-L *et al* (1997) 'An empirical comparison of four generic health status measures: the Nottingham Health Profile, the medical outcomes study 36-Item Short-Form Health Survey, the COOP/WONCA Charts, and the EuroQol Instrument', *Medical Care*, **35** (5), pp 522–37.

Farr, W (1853) 'The income and property tax', *Journal of the Statistical Society*, **16** (1), pp 1–44.

Fein, R (1958) *Economics of Mental Illness*, Basic Books, New York.

Fletcher, A (1995) 'Quality-of-life measurements in the evaluation of treatment: proposed guidelines', *British Journal of Clinical Pharmacology*, **39** (3), pp 217–22.

Fletcher, A *et al* (1992) 'Quality of life measures in health care. II: Design, analysis, and interpretation', *British Medical Journal*, **305** (N), pp 1145–8.

Froberg, DG and Kane, RL (1989) 'Methodology for measuring health-state preferences – II: scaling methods', *Journal of Clinical Epidemiology*, **42** (5), pp 459–71.

Gafni, A (1991) 'Willingness-to-pay as a measure of benefits: relevant questions in the context of public decisionmaking about health care programs', *Medical Care*, **29** (12), pp 1246–52.

Gafni, A and Birch, S (1995) 'Preferences for outcomes in economic evaluation: an economic approach to addressing economic problems', *Social Science and Medicine*, **40** (6), pp 767–76.

Glied, S (1996) 'Estimating the indirect cost of illness: an assessment of the foregone earnings approach', *American Journal of Public Health*, **86** (12), pp 1723–8.

Graham, B and McGregor, K (1997) 'What does a GP consultation cost?', *British Journal of General Practice*, **47** (N), pp 170–2.

Gray, A and Fenn, P (1993) 'Alzheimer's Disease: the burden of the illness in England', *Health Trends*, **25** (1), pp 31–7.

Gray, AM *et al* (1997) 'Problems in conducting economic evaluations alongside clinical trials: lessons from a study of case management for people with mental disorders', *British Journal of Psychiatry*, **170** (1), pp 47–52.

Hadorn, DC (1991) 'Setting health care priorities in Oregon: cost-effectiveness meets the rule of rescue', *Journal of the American Medical Association*, **265** (17), pp 2218–25.

Hall, J *et al* (1992) 'A cost utility analysis of mammography screening in Australia', *Social Science and Medicine*, **34** (9), pp 993–1004.

Halvorsen, PA and Kristiansen, IS (1996) 'Radiology services for remote communities: cost minimisation study of telemedicine', *British Medical Journal*, **312** (N), pp 1333–6.

Hart, JT (1995) 'Clinical and economic consequences of patients as producers', *Journal of Public Health Medicine*, **17** (4), pp 383–6.

Hartunian, NS, Smart, CN and Thompson, MS (1981) *The Incidence and Economic Costs of Major Health Impairments*, Lexington Books, Lexington.

Henke, K-D and Behrens, C (1986) 'The economic cost of illness in the Federal Republic of Germany in the year 1980', *Health Policy*, **6** (2), pp 119–43.

Hodgson, TA and Meiners, MR (1982) 'Cost of illness methodology: a guide to current practices and procedures', *Milbank Memorial Fund Quarterly*, **60** (3), pp 429–62.

Hunt, S, McKenna, SP and McEwen, J (1989) *The Nottingham Health Profile User's Manual*, Galen Research and Consultancy, Manchester.

Hunter, DJ (1996) 'Rationing and evidence-based medicine', *Journal of Evaluation in Clinical Practice*, **2** (1), pp 5–8.

Indredavik, B *et al* (1997) 'Stroke unit treatment: Long term effects', *Stroke*, **28** (10), pp 1861–6.

Jefferson, T *et al* (1996) 'An exercise on the feasibility of carrying out secondary economic analyses', *Health Economics*, **5** (2), pp 155–65.

Johannesson, M and Jönsson, B (1991) 'Economic evaluation in health care: Is there a role for cost-benefit analysis?', *Health Policy*, **17** (1), pp 1–23.

Johannesson, M, Jönsson, B and Karlsson, G (1996) 'Outcome and measurement in economic evaluation', *Health Economics*, **5** (4), pp 279–96.

Johnson, S (1997) 'Dual diagnosis of severe mental illness and substance abuse: a case for specialist services?', *British Journal of Psychiatry*, **171** (9), pp 205–8.

Kenkel, D (1994) 'Cost of illness approach' in *Valuing Health for Policy*, ed G Tolley, D Kenkel and R Fabian, University of Chicago Press, Chicago.

Kind, P *et al* (1998) ' Variations in population health state: results from a United Kingdom national questionnaire survey', *British Medical Journal*, **316** (7133), pp 736–41.

Klein, R (1997) 'Defining a package of healthcare services the NHS is responsible for: The case against', *British Medical Journal*, **314** (7079), pp 506–9.

Knapp, M (1993a) 'Background theory', in *Costing Community Care*, ed A Netten and J Beecham, Ashgate, Aldershot.

Knapp, M (1993b) 'Principles of applied cost research', in *Costing Community Care*, ed A Netten and J Beecham, Ashgate, Aldershot.

Knapp, MRJ and Beecham, J (1990) 'Costing mental health services', *Psychological Medicine*, **20** (4), pp 893–908.

Knapp, M and Beecham, J (1993) 'Reduced list costings: examination of an informed short cut in mental health research', *Health Economics*, **2** (4), pp 313–22.

Koopmanschap, MA and van Ineveld, BM (1992) 'Towards a new approach for estimating indirect costs of disease', *Social Science and Medicine*, **34** (9), pp 1005–10.

Krahn, M and Gafni, A (1993) 'Discounting in the economic evaluation of health care interventions', *Medical Care*, **31** (5), pp 403–18.

La Croix, SJ and Russo, G (1996) 'A cost-benefit analysis of voluntary routine HIV-antibody testing for hospital patients', *Social Science and Medicine*, **42** (9), pp 1259–72.

Langfitt, JT (1997) 'Cost-effectiveness of anterotemporal lobectomy in medically intractable complex partial epilepsy', *Epilepsy*, **38** (2), pp 154–63.

Light, DW (1997) 'The real ethics of rationing', *British Medical Journal*, **315** (7100), pp 112–15.

Ludbrook, A and Mooney, G (1984) *Economic Appraisal in the NHS: Problems and Challenges*, Northern Health Economics, Aberdeen.

Maki, DG *et al* (1997) 'Prevention of central venous catheter-related blood-stream infection by use of an antiseptic-impregnated catheter. A random-ized, controlled trial', *Annals of International Medicine*, **127** (4), pp 257–66.

Malone, DC *et al* (1997) 'A cost of illness study of allergic rhinitis in the United States', *Journal of Allergy and Clinical Immunology*, **99** (1), pp 22–7.

Malzberg, B (1950) 'Mental illness and the economic value of a man', *Mental Hygiene*, **34** (4), pp 582–91.

Mason, J, Drummond, M and Torrance, G (1993) 'Some guidelines on the use of cost-effectiveness league tables', *British Medical Journal*, **306** (6877), pp 570–2.

McGuire, A, Henderson, J and Mooney, G (1988) *The Economics of Health Care: An Introductory Text*, Routledge, London.

McHorney, CA, Ware, JE and Raczek, AE (1993) 'The MOS 36-item Short-Form Health Survey (SF-36). II. Psychometric and clinical tests of validity in measuring physical and mental health constructs', *Medical Care*, **31** (N), pp 247–63.

Mehrez, A and Gafni, A (1989) 'Quality adjusted life years, utility theory, and healthy-years equivalents', *Medical Decision Making*, **9** (2), pp 142–9.

Mooney, G (1992) *Economics, Medicine and Health Care*, 2nd edn, Harvester Wheatsheaf, London.

Muller, A and Reutzel, TJ (1984) 'Willingness to pay for reduction in fatality risk: an exploratory survey', *American Journal of Public Health*, **74** (8), pp 808–11.

Murray, CJL (1994) 'Quantifying the burden of disease: the technical basis of disability-adjusted life years', *Bulletin of the World Health Organization*, **72** (3), pp 429–45.

Netten, A and Dennett, J (1997) *Unit Costs of Health and Social Care*, Personal Social Services Research Unit, Canterbury.

Neuhauser, D and Lewicki, A (1975) 'What do we gain from the sixth stool guaiac?', *New England Journal of Medicine*, **293** (5), pp 226–8.

New, B (1997) 'Defining a package of healthcare services the NHS is responsi-ble for: The case for', *British Medical Journal*, **314** (7079), pp 503–5.

Nord, E (1992) 'An alternative to QALYs: the saved young life equivalent (SAVE)', *British Medical Journal*, **305** (6858), pp 875–7.

Nord, E (1992) 'Methods for quality adjustment of life years', *Social Science and Medicine*, **34** (5), pp 559–69.

Normand, C (1991) 'Economics, health, and the economics of health', *British Medical Journal*, **303** (6817), pp 1572–7.

Olsen, JA and Donaldson, C (1998) 'Helicopters, hearts and hips: using will-ingness to pay to set priorities for public health care programmes', *Social Science and Medicine*, **46** (1), pp 1–12.

Osmond, MH, Klassen, TP and Quinn, JV (1995) 'Economic comparison of a tissue adhesive and suturing in the repair of pediatric facial lacerations', *Journal of Pediatrics*, **126** (6), pp 892–5.

Oyebode, F (1994) 'Ethics and resource allocation: can health care outcomes be QALYfied?', *Psychiatric Bulletin*, **18** (7), pp 395–8.

Polychronis, A, Miles, A and Bentley, P (1996) 'Evidence-based medicine: Reference? Dogma? Neologism? New orthodoxy?', *Journal of Evaluation in Clinical Evaluation*, **2** (1), pp 1–3.

Popkin, BM *et al* (1980) 'Benefit-cost analysis in the nutrition area: a project in the Philippines', *Social Science and Medicine*, **14C** (3), pp 207–16.

Rapier, CM and Hutchinson, DR (1995) 'How useful are the UK guidelines for reviewing manuscripts submitted for publication?', *British Journal of Medical Economics*, **8** (3), pp vii–xiii.

Reinhardt, UE (1997) 'Making economic evaluation respectable', *Social Science and Medicine*, **45** (40), pp 555–62.

Rice, DP (1966) *Estimating the Cost of Illness*, Health Economic Series no 6, US Department of Health, Education, and Welfare, Washington DC.

Rice, DP (1967) 'Estimating the cost of illness', *American Journal of Public Health*, **57** (3), pp 424–40.

Richardson, J (1994) 'Cost-utility analysis: what should be measured?' *Social Science and Medicine*, **39** (1), pp 7–21.

Robinson, R (1993) 'Costs and cost-minimisation analysis', *British Medical Journal*, **307** (6906), pp 726–8.

Rosser, R *et al* (1992) 'Index of health-related quality of life', in *Measures of the Quality of Life and the Use to which such Measures may be Used*, ed A Hopkins, Royal College of Physicians, London.

Royce, R (1993) 'DRGs and the internal market', *British Journal of Healthcare Computing*, February, pp 27–8.

Ryan, M (1993) *Valuing the Benefits of Health Care: Conjoint Analysis or Contingent Valuation?*, Health Economics Research Unit Discussion Paper No 02/93, University of Aberdeen, Aberdeen.

Ryan, M, Ratcliffe, J and Tucker, J (1997) 'Using willingness to pay to value alternative models of antenatal care', *Social Science and Medicine*, **44** (3), pp 371–80.

Ryynänen, O-P *et al* (1996) 'Random paired scenarios – a method for investigating attitudes to prioritisation in medicine', *Journal of Medical Ethics*, **22** (4), pp 238–42.

Sackett, DL and Haynes, RB (1995) 'On the need for evidence-based medicine', *Evidence-Based Medicine*, **1** (1), pp 5–6.

Sackett, DL *et al* (1996) 'Evidence based medicine: what it is and what it isn't', *British Medical Journal*, **312** (7023), pp 71–2.

Serafetinides (1991) 'Cost of psychiatric illness versus cost of psychiatric research' [letter], *American Journal of Psychiatry*, **148** (7), p 951.

Sheldon, TA (1996) 'Problems of using modelling in the economic evaluation of health care', *Health Economics*, **5** (1), pp 1–11.

Shiell, A, Gerard, K and Donaldson, C (1987) 'Cost of illness studies: an aid to decision-making?', *Health Policy*, **8** (3), pp 317–23.

Smith, K and Wright, K (1996) 'Costs of mental illness in Britain', *Health Policy*, **35** (1), pp 61–73.

Spoor, C, Mooney, G and Maynard, A (1986) 'Teaching health economics',

British Medical Journal, **292** (6523), p 785.

Stavem, K (1998) 'Quality of life in epilepsy: comparison of four preference measures', *Epilepsy Research*, **29** (3), pp 201–9.

Thompson, MS (1986) 'Willingness to pay and accept risks to cure chronic disease', *American Journal of Public Health*, **76** (4), pp 392–6.

Torrance, GW, Sackett, DL and Thomas, WH (1972) 'A utility maximisation model for program evaluation of health care programs', *Health Services Research*, **7** (2), pp 118–33.

Tousignant, P *et al* (1994) 'Quality adjusted life years added by treatment of obstructive sleep apnea', *Sleep*, **17** (1), pp 52–60.

Varian, HR (1987) *Intermediate Microeconomics*, Norton, New York.

Ware, JE and Sherbourne, CD (1992) 'The MOS 36-item Short-Form Health Survey (SF-36). I. Conceptual framework and item selection', *Medical Care*, **30** (6), pp 473–83.

Weinstein, MC and Stason, WB (1977) 'Foundations of cost-effectiveness analysis for health and medical practices', *New England Journal of Medicine*, **296** (13), pp 716–21.

Whynes, DK and Walker, AR (1995) 'On approximations in treatment costing', *Health Economics*, **4** (1), pp 31–9.

Williams, A (1974) 'The cost-benefit approach', *British Medical Bulletin*, **30** (3), pp 252–6.

Wolff, N, Helminiak, TW and Tebes, JK (1997) 'Getting the cost right in cost-effectiveness analyses', *American Journal of Psychiatry*, **154** (6), pp 736–43.

Index